P

Rick Wehler was one of the most creative minds I ever met in the produce industry. Rick's passion behind produce and quick wit made him a fan favorite among produce managers and field specialists alike. I used to always love reading Rick's..."You might be a Veg Man if" quotes. Here's one of my favorites: "YOU MIGHT BE A VEG MAN IF: YOU CAN'T KEEP FROM STRAIGHTENING THE DISPLAYS WHEN YOU ARE SHOPPING OR EVEN WHEN IN THE COMPETITION." I cannot wait to read Rick's book. I am certain it will create a tummy-ache from laughing so hard. I am very lucky to call Rick a friend and a mentor.
—Jim Sarcletti, Director of Produce, Supervalu's West Region, Hopkins, MN

###

I have always enjoyed reading Rick's stories. Although we are many miles apart, it's amazing to see the parallels in our lives within his stories. I am confident that had Rick and I lived closer, we would have grown up being best friends.
—George Randall (Rick's younger cousin) Granby, MA

###

Rick's stories are delightful. He has an uncanny ability to see the humor in most any situation and is able through his writing to bring you along for the adventure, much like the style of Patrick F. McManus. Love, love the Turkey Bingo story! Read his stories and you will undoubtedly see yourself in many of the experiences, or wish you were there.
—Lorraine Scott, Retired Science Teacher, Damascus, OR

###

What Rick has written is true. At least most of it. OR That tree I dropped on him grew longer on the way down. OR Being married to the Norwegian girl for so long, Rick has the right to fabricate a few facts. —Glen Rosio, retired Director of Purchasing, Richland Center, WI

###

Rick is a fantastic writer with such wit and charm! I love reading about his adventures while he was the "Veg Man," and tales of the love of his life, Cora, "The Dish"! Some of his stories about going to the doctor had me laughing out loud. A must read!
—Rose M. Davis, Floral Manager-Cub Foods, Freeport, IL

###

Good writers have the ability to transform the mundane into something quite interesting. Add in an incisive sense of humor and a sharp wit and you have what Rick is able to create. Thank you, Rick for the steady stream of most enjoyable vignettes. And all my best to Cora "the Dish," whom I suspect is a saint. —Al Vignieri, Orchardist, Richland Center, WI

###

Rick Wehler is a clever, witty, funny, wry writer. His off-the-wall humor always surfaces a chuckle and often a corresponding raised eyebrow. —Dr. Terry Hadlock, Wilsonville, OR

North of Normal

Minne-Sconsin Stories

NORTH OF NORMAL
Minne-Sconsin Stories

Rick A. Wehler

Milwaukee, Wisconsin

Copyright © 2016 by Rick A. Wehler
All rights reserved.

Some names have been changed to protect people's privacy.

Published by
HenschelHAUS Publishing, Inc.
www.henschelHAUSbooks.com

ISBN: 978-159598-458-6
E-ISBN: 978159598-459-3
Library of Congress Control Number (LCCN): 2016933749

Printed in the United States of America

This book is dedicated to my wife, Cora, "the Dish," who has kept my Minne-Sconsin humor alive.

Table of Contents

Preface i
Turkey Bingo, Norwegian Style 1
Incinerator 5
Instruction in Comedic Writing 101xy 9
It's Good to Have Family 11
Cauliflower 18
Chanel #5 20
Jeopardy 24
Clark 26
Cable Services for Free 33
Fresh Air 36
Tick and Dick 40
El Diablo 42
An Innocent Bet 43
A Dish of Norwegian Crow 48
Lunch TMI 51
Preamble / A Singular Leather Jacket 56
Forget About It 64
King George I Vignettes 67
Sharing the Covers 72
Now That's Just Not Fair 74
Romance in Bloom 80
A Bedtime Primer: May You Rest in Peace 82
Subterranean 88
Sup and Spew 92
Warsh 94
The View 99
Cholesterol Count 100
No More Tears 104
Caste Not 107
Special Occasions 113
The Buzz 115

Acknowledgements 119
About the Author 121

Preface

My wife, Cora "the Dish," and I purchased our first desktop computer in 1998. It was a monster! Together we hefted the monitor and keyboard up onto a padded oak desk, and made room for the tower by donating our loveseat to a thrift store.

My baby sister, Ru, and I began swapping emails, making fun of life and each other religiously. I found writing, laced with what "the Dish" has called "a weird sense of humor" to be down-right therapeutic.

Through writing, I've learned how to laugh at the challenges of life in Minne-Sconsin, most notably jobs, hobbies, humdrum happenings, health headaches, foibles, family, friends, fond memories, doctors and nurses, and psychotic states of mind induced by the consumption of copious quantities of complex sugars.

It's my hope that each reader will be able to identify with one of the short stories that follow—a paragraph, a sentence, or a character—and laugh along with me.

Rick Wehler

TURKEY BINGO, NORWEGIAN STYLE

My wife, Cora, and I had chosen the weekend before Thanksgiving to visit her Ma, her brother Richie, and his fiancée Debby in their Northern Minnesota hometown, population 1,000, rife with Norwegians.

Upon our arrival, Ma informed us of the family events for that evening: a heart-healthy meal of the best broasted chicken around, lovingly prepared by the gourmet chefs at the Deer Creek Feed and Bleed, followed by the V.F.W. Turkey Bingo Fund Raiser.

After gobbling all the fowl we could stuff, our group proceeded to the Community Center in time for the gaming. Even though my poor luck at gambling had become family folklore, I did not wish to earn an additional rep as party pooper and agreed to attend the function.

The building's interior was crammed wall-to-wall with lunchroom-type tables, a myriad of clanking metal folding chairs and hundreds of local residents. I could not help but wonder who was milking the cows. Due to the overflow turnout, several sought-after chairs up front uncomfortably accommodated more than one backside each.

At an entrance table Ma purchased the use of one well-used bingo card for each of us, although some of the patrons purchased as many as five cards.

We found an unoccupied table with no chairs by the back door. Upon our request, one of the V.F.W. regulars recruited five chairs, which he had found hidden out back in the shed. He tramped our way in his jingling, unbuckled rubber boots, fur hat with ear flaps and dangling straps, foggy glasses, well-worn, wet work gloves and an open jacket. He leaned the frost-covered metal folding chairs against our table and accepted our thanks.

All of the event's officials were located way up in front: Hilde, the bingo machine operator, dressed in a flowered blouse with a flamboyant breast pin, Einar, the announcer, bedecked in his V.F.W. hat bedizened with multiple awards, and Olga, the game's judge, who sported transparent nasal air tubes, which led into an oxygen tank hidden under the table.

I learned from Einar's announcement that I was to endure 15 bingo games that evening. Previous to this, I was willingly ignorant of the many different bingo versions—regular bingo, 4-corners bingo, X-bingo, picture frame bingo and black-out bingo. I felt certain that my fabled ill-fortune would continue.

Games 1 through 4 passed uneventfully. All winners were somewhere within Olga's hearing. Several losers traded in their unlucky cards in hopes of finding one with inherent good fortune. I felt no need to trade my card and reduce my meager chances to zero, like the temperature of my hinder.

Game 5 produced a winner at our table as Richie yelled, "Bingo." The rules required the judge to authenticate his winning numbers. Mr. Jingling Boot Buckles was kind enough to act on Olga's behalf. Yup, Richie's victory was confirmed. Mr. Ear Flaps opened the back door, retrieved Richie's prize from the bed of a pickup truck and dropped an 11 lb. turkey on our table with an ice cracking thud. We sensed the envious stares from the multiple-card-holding occupants of adjacent tables.

Game 7, a four-corner game in which the winner must— oh, just figure it out—was won by Ma. (None of my four corners participated.) Mr. Foggy Glasses repeated the verification and turkey presentation. Our frozen table guest, the turkey, now had a mate. I didn't fret about hanky-panky on their part. I

Turkey Bingo, Norwegian Style

believe that frozen turkeys are neutered. We again bore the gaze of jealous rivals.

As Game 8 commenced, I finally found employment for a few of my game tokens upon the bingo card. What, four in a row? Why that's almost a winner!

I stared at the column's remaining uncovered position, O-69. I concentrated on the cipher. I moved my lips and spoke it silently, attempting to hypnotize Einar from afar. As I once again mouthed 0-69, I did so in unison with Einar. *Wha, wha, what? I, I, won.* "Bingo!" Oh, yes, Olga heard me alright. A legion of tonight's neglected cows in a hundred abandoned barns mooed in praise of my accomplishment.

Mr. Well-Worn, Wet Work Gloves once again verified the triumphant numbers and plunked another turkey onto our table. In geometry, three points determine a plane. In this bingo hall, three turkeys nearly fomented a riot.

The mood settled a bit as game 9 began. I followed along, even though I was shivering from my chilly chair, the continued icy wind blasts from the back door, the fog radiating from the thawing turkeys, the competitor's cold stares and my recent good luck. OMG, I filled another full line! *Dare I, should I, oh why not?* Freaking "BINGO!" I have no doubt that several people at nearby tables soiled themselves. I am fairly sure that I did. Mr. Open Jacket followed his proven procedure with a little extra thunk. We then owned 43 pounds of frozen fowl.

The following game, a blackout—cover all the numbers—was won elsewhere, as were games 11 and 12. Game 13, however, was a game that will live in the annals of V.F.W. Turkey Bingo history, as Cora screamed, "Bingo!" Never before had one small group of contestants won so many games.

By now our team was on a first-name basis with our V.F.W. assistant, Jingles, his preferred moniker. He leaned against the building's back wall with his arms and boots crossed and smiled as he watched the melt water drip from our 54 pound prodigious poultry pile while the final two games were won by other contenders.

We left our lucky bingo cards on the table as Jingles enabled our escape through the back door with our five thawing turkeys and five frozen fannies.

#####

INCINERATOR

Marv was my boss, my very first boss, not counting my parents. At 5 foot 10 inches tall, with a trim build, wavy brown hair and a mischievous smile, he had all the makings to drive women wild and me nuts. We worked together in a small, suburban Minneapolis grocery store during the winter of 1966/67. That is, I worked. He gave orders and messed with all the women.

"Rick, go burn the cardboard," Marv ordered.

I mumbled, "Oh, hell. I hate that job." I could say "hell" because my mom wasn't there and Marv said lots worse than that. Marv removed the cigar stub from the corner of his mouth and repeated the command in such language that Mom was sure to know if I even thought those words.

The incinerator was just outside and to the right of the store's cinder-block back wall and metal-reinforced backdoor. It was cylindrical, measured about 8 feet wide by 8 feet tall, with a chimney that rose another 15 feet or so. You might think that the door to the burner's insides would be humongous, but no: it was more like the door to a Franklin wood stove. That made putting a toilet tissue box into the fire a real challenge.

The entire contraption was enclosed by a protective, sheet-metal fence that had been brand spanking new about 15 years ago. Its chimney was just tall enough to shoot the ash out of the parking lot and into the neighbors' yards. Most of them hadn't seen white snow in years.

I glommed onto the protective parka that Marv had found in the trash and set aside just for burning cardboard. It sported more holes than fabric and most of the stuffing had been sacrificed to the fire at one time or another. Donning the parka reminded me of the biblical sackcloth and ashes because the other unlucky guys who had this job never bothered to clean it.

"Hell, I forgot my head gear," I cursed at no one in particular. I grabbed a plastic bag, drenched it in tap water and pulled it on over my hair. Now properly protected, I tackled the first obstacle—lighting the fire. That was no small feat since the flaming thing had never been cleaned out. But I was the best firebug in the area and the only clear choice for this assignment. (I had once started a fire in my schoolyard softball field using dried leaves and my left eyeglass as a magnifier. Another time, I burned down a hollow tree in the field behind our house during a thunderstorm. Lightning was to blame, according to the firemen.)

I told myself, "It's time to get this baby fired up. Dig a hole in the soot and jam in some kindling." My favorite tinder was a combination of Marv's apron that he set aside whenever he went for a coffee break, a frequent occurrence, and gas that I siphoned from his 1966 muscle car. Within a few minutes, I had the fire cooking and my thick glasses were coated with ash. Although it was nighttime, I hardly knew it because the sides of the incinerator were glowing.

When stuck with this job, I always made sure to have a hunk of bubble gum to chew so I could produce plenty of spit, hock a gob onto the burner's side and listen to it sizzle. Tonight that just wasn't enough action, so I stuffed the burner until the chimney glowed.

Within half an hour, the chimney was seething in multi-colors nearly to the top, well beyond my previous record height. It then began to warp. The sparks and ash were shooting 20 degrees south of vertical and arcing right into Old Lady Huebner's backyard. I reasoned, "If her dog starts howling, she'll call the cops for sure. Well, what the hell? If I'm going to get fired, I might as well go out with a bang."

INCINERATOR

I walked over to the garbage dumpster and dug out a gold mine of damaged aerosol cans. I widened the hole into the fire with a strip of molding that had fallen off of the side of our butcher's clunker, bit the nozzles off of several hairspray cans as if they were hand grenades, pitched them into Dante's inferno, and slammed closed the metal door. I didn't make it out of the enclosure before a *THWANG* hammered my ears. The incinerator door had burst open, thanks to the force created by a week's worth of burning trash, dented cans, unlabeled glass jars, and exploding aerosol cans.

One of the hairspray cans, now a Russian guided missile, spiraled a couple feet toward me right out of the shoot, and then shot straight up about half way to the Big Dipper. Unfortunately, it didn't escape the Earth's gravity and came down instead on top of Old Lady Huebner's doghouse roof. Her dog let out a *HHAAAOOOO*, as if someone had shot it in the tail with a pellet gun. It took off doing 60 mph on a 10-foot chain bolted to the house. Fortunately, the doghouse wasn't nailed down—it followed that dog wherever it led. Don't know where they went. Didn't inquire.

The incinerator missile reminded me a lot of last summer's Fourth of July celebration, when Jerry and I shot cherry bombs over the pond in front of my house using a sling shot. I held the bomb in the pouch and stretched back the strap of inner-tube rubber, while Jerry lit the fuse.

Then *WHOOANG!* I shot it up thousands of feet into the night sky. The cherry bomb exploded like Zeus's own thunder (I learned about Zeus and Dante in Miss Fine Body's literature class, where I paid close attention) and echoed from here to my Dad's bedroom.

Questions filled my mind. "Why couldn't Dad for once blame something on Davy, my next door neighbor? How come

Dad never hears Mom when she blows up? She's louder than any cherry bomb."

Now what do I do? Cool, I've got half a dozen aerosol cans left over, but first things first. I've got to put out the burning junk that spattered all over my back.

I dropped onto the snow-covered alleyway and made one of the best snow angels you ever saw, complete with plastic bag halo. Marv opened the back door, saw me squirming on the ground, and demanded, "Rick, stop screwing around and get your tail in here. Some old fart dropped a jar of sauerkraut in aisle number three."

Early the next morning, the chimney resembled my dad's spine, looking left and pointing right. Old Lady Huebner was standing on her back stoop with her hair wrapped up in a turban, wearing bedroom slippers and holding closed a bathrobe that made our incinerator coat look classy. She was calling for her dog, "Oh, Precious! Oh, Precious! Where are you? It's time for breakfast, Snookems."

Marv, always the one to ruin the moment, barged out and yelled, "Rick, stop dinking around and go help that fat broad carry out her groceries."

#####

INSTRUCTION IN COMEDIC WRITING 101xy

Composing a self-described humorous anecdote need not be a trying task. Upon arising at 4:30 a.m. subsequent to a satisfying night's sabbatical—a five-hour slumber uninterrupted by baby babbling, cat carousing, dream dread, night noises, refrigerator revenge, spousal snoring, work worries, or urinary urges—well, okay, three hours, dine on a hearty breakfast consisting of a pot of espresso, a carafe of Sunny Delight, and three heaping bowls full of Super Sugar Smacks.

Prepare accordingly during the approximately thirty-seven minutes and twelve seconds of sanity before the maniacal, caffeinated sugar buzz strikes. I recommend a comfortable computer chair restraint and a super-size pack of paper products for managing profuse sweating, copious saliva, and other inappropriate, but understandable, fluidic responses.

Plan to practice patience while keyboarding as symptomatic shaking fingers are most exasperating. The challenge will then be to select a single subject from the battling barrage of fancies assaulting your common sense and concentrate solely upon the chosen one.

Resist the temptation to consume your child's A.D.D. medication. If you find the need to refuel during your writing frenzy, I recommend a peanut butter, clover honey and marshmallow cream sandwich on healthy whole wheat bread.

Inscribe your first draft hurriedly before the inevitable caffeinated, complex carbohydrate crash. If you act swiftly, disparate ideas will congeal in a fashion not imagined by

Rowan and Martin, Ricky Martin, Martin Landau, Martin Luther or Martini and Rossi-prohibiting Protestants.

Have close at hand a current Thesaurus and a reference book on phraseology. They will prove to be especially helpful in demonstrating your keen intellect by upgrading word choices, such as understanding to perspicacious or replacing aphorisms with considerate reactions, for instance replace "go piss up a rope" with "I don't agree with you." Unfortunate readers familiar with your inherent mental acuity will be particularly amused. At a later date, you will marvel that such irrational thoughts were created within your sensible psyche and were able to be recorded during your inter-dimensional travels.

Defy the desire to activate your computer's delete option and erase your shame. Humor is often times created by connecting incongruent thoughts that an untroubled individual might not have correlated. Hopefully, the reader will find the union amusing. If you are at the high end of the sugar-induced bipolar roller coaster, you may not much care if the readers make the intended associations or not in which case you might advise them to go piss up a rope.

Submit your comedic triumph to a few close friends, if you have any remaining, for their honest scrutiny. Consider their observations and promptly dismiss them as mere jealous rants. Enjoy your completed work. Lastly and of the utmost importance, do not, under any circumstances, invite your spouse's literary appraisal.

#####

It's Good to Have Family

Three days before my surgery, grandson Noah, age 18, sent me an email that asked, "Grandpa, have you written down your secret recipe for a homemade, chocolate, banana, root beer milkshake, just in case your surgery goes wrong?"

It's good to have family.

Recently, my urologist, Dr. Sherman Peabody, discovered I had kidney cancer and recommended a laparoscopic, hand-assisted, radical nephrectomy.

I reflected, "That's an impressive term, but it hardly seems fair to have such a malady. I don't drink, smoke, do drugs or take medications. I'm physically fit. I chase women, but I never catch them. I should be perfectly healthy."

Even though the procedure and the possible side effects, such as death, didn't scare me, I decided to get a hair cut. I figured, "If I'm going to be dead, then I'm going to look good!"

To avoid disquieting medical terminology, I'll paraphrase Dr. Peabody's pre-surgical instructions:

- On the day before your surgery, eat only bland foods, such as Jell-O or soup broth.
- Then at about 6 p.m., take a laxative called magnesium citrate. It's available over the counter at any drugstore.
- After your surgery, you will stay in the hospital for two nights or until you make a reasonable bathroom deposit.

I couldn't help but think, and this isn't paraphrased, "If you expect me to take a dump after an intestinal flush and within

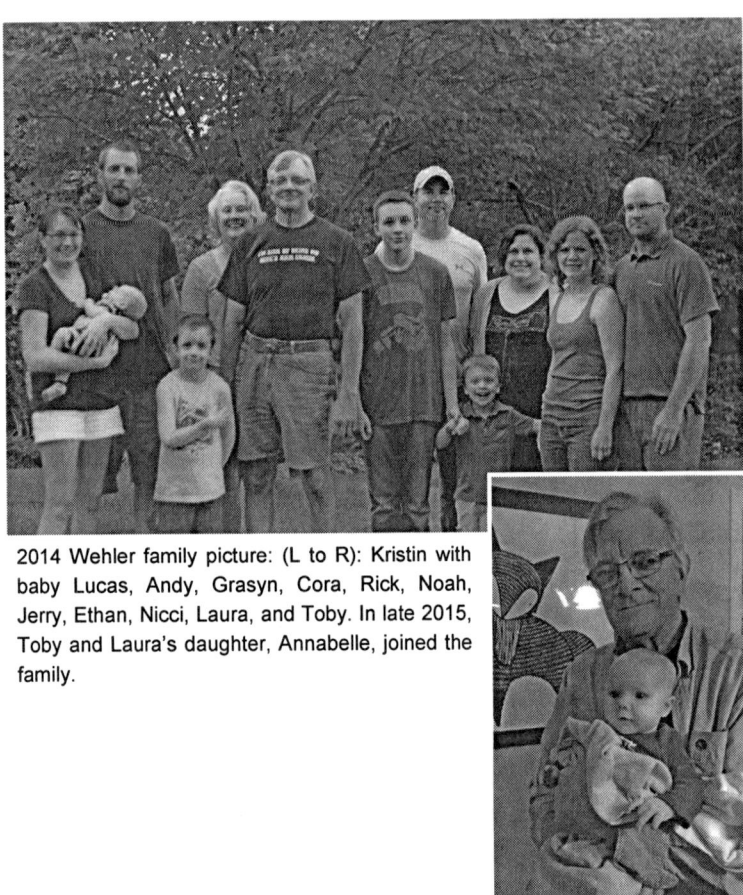

2014 Wehler family picture: (L to R): Kristin with baby Lucas, Andy, Grasyn, Cora, Rick, Noah, Jerry, Ethan, Nicci, Laura, and Toby. In late 2015, Toby and Laura's daughter, Annabelle, joined the family.

two days after surgery, then I'd better be allowed to eat something with more guts than Jell-O or soup broth."

At 6 b.m., I held before me the bottle of magnesium citrate that I had purchased from a Walgreen's pharmacist, Mr. Squatter. The instructions stated, "Normal dose: ½ bottle." Wishing to be thorough, I downed the entire jug. About three hours later, my insides churned as if I'd soon birth a litter of aliens. Without going into specifics, I'll just say that the outcome would have made Montezuma proud.

It's Good to Have Family

July 1st 2014 was my kidney's day of destiny. Cora and I entered the hospital at 5:45 a.m. to prepare for the 7:30 a.m. procedure. We checked in with a representative at the front desk. She asked my name and birth date, compared it to her records and directed us towards the surgical department. Throughout my stay, I recited my name and birth date so often that by the time we headed for home, I had them fairly well committed to memory.

A surgical nurse escorted us to a semi-public room and handed me six individually wrapped XXXL alcohol wipes. She pointed towards a chart: the silhouette of a man, both front and back sides, pinned to the wall, with body sections numbered and color coded. (That chart brought back a few early marriage memories.)

The nurse requested that Cora and I scrub me down using one sheet for each numbered and colored coded area. I stripped and asked Cora, "Will you handle area #1 blue please?"

She replied, "Only if these are Brillo pads."

Germ-free and unfulfilled, I donned a backside-challenged surgical robe and awaited further instructions.

Fifty-three minutes later, the anesthesiologist, Dr. Cy Lent, and the tour guide, Nurse Gurney, arrived. Dr. Cy implanted numerous IVs in the back of my left arm, each one with an apology for the puncture pain. I kissed Cora good-bye, but I couldn't reach my ass or my kidney.

As Nurse Gurney wheeled me down the halls, I found the passing ceiling lights highly reminiscent of TV medical dramas. Within the operating theater, I counted seven medical staff, Dr. Peabody, his resident Dr. House, Dr. Cy Lent, Nurse Gurney and three nameless surgical techs of varying genders. Two of the crew lifted me onto an operating table equipped with ankle shackles. I couldn't help but think, "If this was under other circumstances…"

I don't remember waking up, but I'm fairly certain that I did. I postulated, "I'm alive and about 60 percent aware. If that's true, then I'm within 15 percent of normal. Hallelujah."

The rest of the day and night I spent on an angled bed connected to IVs, medical instruments with backup beepers and a catheter. I smiled and spoke to myself, "Cool, I don't have to get out of bed to take a leak. It's just as well. With my right kidney gone, I'd probably only be able to whiz to the left. That could cause targeting problems. At least I've still got my sense of humor and potty mouth. Losing either one of those would've pissed me off."

The next morning at about 7 a.m., Nurse Zeb stopped in to prep me for a walk about. He instructed, "Grit your teeth while I remove this catheter." While he was so employed, I complained within, "Where the hell's the end of it? If you keep this up, I'm going to lose another urinary appliance. I've got bruises in so many places, including the former host of that catheter. Did Dr. Peabody hang me up by those ankle shackles and operate while I was flopping around like a fresh-caught bluegill?"

Without comment, Nurse Zeb then helped me out of bed.

I bragged, "My wife likes me to wear hospital gowns so she can ogle my butt."

Cora jibed, "You've got no butt to ogle."

Nurse Zeb ordered, "Put on this robe so you're not mooning the public."

I retorted, "So just like Cora, you don't feel they'd be impressed. Isn't there anybody out there who appreciates a work of art?"

By the time I returned from our walk, I'd developed an appetite. I asked Zeb, "Does this place serve bacon or crab legs?" I don't remember what I didn't eat, but I do remember that it wasn't crispy and there wasn't any melted butter.

Later that morning, our son Andy and his wife Kristin stopped by for a visit. Their son Lucas had been born the night before in the same hospital. I had known of Lucas's birth before my surgery and found it comforting. If things went wrong for me, I'd have a replacement who wouldn't covet my milkshake recipe.

Andy commented, "I hope what they removed from you didn't weigh as much as Lucas."

At 4 p.m., Dr. Peabody stopped by to check on my progress.

I said, "Thanks for all that your team did for me."

He replied, "You're welcome."

I asked, "Is my treatment complete?"

He replied, "Yes."

I asserted, "Then I'm going home. I can rest just as well there and it's a lot cheaper. I don't know what my hospital bill will amount to, but I'm sure it'll be a pisser."

Cora drove me home, doing her level best to avoid potholes.

I crowed, "Just one night in the hospital and I'm already home. I'll be doing my thing long before you grant me permission. For my first lunch, I'll have a homemade, chocolate, banana, root beer milkshake and two pieces of cake. Hey, I could've been dead. Life is sweet!"

Cora suggested that I sleep upon my back for the utmost comfort. She equipped our recliner with blankets, a heating pad for my back, ice packs for the incisions on my stomach, beverages, and the TV remote.

Cora commanded, "To avoid incision pains, you must refrain from sneezing, coughing, belching, hiccupping, laughing, alcohol, and women."

I mumbled, "Alcohol and women? That's just unkind."

The following day, in my stead, our son Jerry mowed the lawn. Cora thanked him and Jerry replied, "I'll come up and cut the grass whenever Dad has a major organ removed. I suggest that he choose wisely. I'm glad to help and happy to hear he's improving. Improving is good, but I'm not sure it is in anyone's best interest for him to be just like before."

It's good to have family.

PEE S.

On July 24th, Dr. Peabody halfheartedly released me to pursue my hazardous hobbies: weightlifting, bike riding, forestry, and chasing the wife.

Cora commented, "One of those undertakings could lead to extensive bruising, dismemberment, or kidney failure."

Yes, yes, it is.

PEE PEE S.

I wrote this thoughtful homage the night before my surgery.

An Ode to My Kidney

You've always had my back.
You've always managed #1.
You've always bailed me out.

Today I'm drinking for two
As tomorrow I bid thee adieu.
With this pre-surgery laxative
My intestines may precede you.

I have a right to be peeved.
I can no longer be relieved.
As you will soon pass away
Know that urine my thoughts.

# # # # #

AFTERTHOUGHTS

Noah posted, "Twinkies are 68 percent air, fact."
I posted, "Noah, you're 68 percent water."
Noah replied, "Grandpa, you're 100 percent old."
Cora said, "I knew I liked that kid."

#

I complained to Cora, "Every time you walk your sultry self by, you crash my thought train."

She replied, "There aren't many cars to derail on your horn-dog express. It doesn't even have a caboose."

#

Jerry, while showing me the interior of his new truck requested, "Hey, Dad, have a look at the back-up camera monitor."

There was Andy mooning me.

It's good to have family.

#

Cauliflower

Sunday morning, we decided to treat our extended family to a dinner of grilled beef tenderloin with side dishes of petite potatoes and various veggies. I thawed the tenderloin, marinated it with sundry spices and allowed it to cure for the afternoon.

That evening, as we served ourselves fillets of beef, Cora lifted the lid on the steamed broccoli and cauliflower and shouted, "Who wants broc and cauk?" Cora knew a split second after the question had flown from her lips that she'd misspoken.

Everyone shook with suppressed laughter, including our three-year-old grandson, who was unaware of the cause. I laughed myself nearly to exhaustion, extinguished suddenly by Cora's glare and certain threatening motions with her lethal ladle.

I, the frequent recipient of Cora's witticisms, patiently awaited the ideal moment to take advantage of her faux pas. In due course, Cora placed two fillets of tenderloin upon her plate.

I then tawdrily asked, "Cora, would you care for a sizable serving of cauliflower to accompany your tender loins?" I should've waited until after Cora set down her carving knife.

The family erupted in laughter, compounded by our grandson's innocent cry, "Nama loves cauliflower."

#####

CAULIFLOWER

AFTERTHOUGHTS

While Cora was preparing fresh vegetables for dinner, I said, "Something doesn't smell right."

She replied, "You're just standing to close to yourself."

I followed up with another comment, to which Cora replied, "Ah, baa-low-nee."

In disbelief, I said, "Did you just say, 'Ah, blow me'?"

In response, she cracked me on the head with her ladle.

#

CHANEL #5

Despite my city boy upbringing, I do enjoy gardening. The confines of our suburban home parcel allow little more than a small patch of ground for such a pursuit. In our neighborhood of well-groomed people and yards, the mish-mash of a garden is not generally appreciated. My best defense has been a sharing attitude.

Raspberries and Concord grapes are my crops of choice. Both are most generous in rewarding even "dead-beat-dad" care. The fruits are delicious, and like insects, the raspberry plants reproduce at an astounding rate.

My first planting of eight bare-root raspberry plants yielded numerous offspring the following season. Many of the progeny met a cruel demise when they escaped the confines of the garden by tunneling to apparent freedom in the lawn beyond the garden's rock wall. As the fleeing raspberry plants reconnoitered just above grass level, they were mercilessly cut down and mulched by one of Toro's best.

Raspberries and Concord grapes, the seeded reward of my labor, are not much to the liking of my dentition. Their seeds seek habitation in the spaces between my teeth with the same zeal as mice in barn wall notches. If not for the joy of watching the plants thrive like so many children, I might have found the cost of dental floss prohibitive.

I planted the grape vines in the proximity of an adult Norway maple. Mr. Norway, even though outdone in total offspring by the raspberries, was proud of his only child growing close by in the garden's rock wall. The concord vines and the young maple without an arbiter made a symbiotic agreement of sorts, and grew nicely together, for a time matching each other's growth in height and in foliage density.

(I am envious of the Concord vines wishing I might entwine about my Norwegian spouse without negotiations.)

After a few seasons, the grape vines climbed from Norway Junior's highest reaches into Dad's outstretched arms, creating an uncommon bond between father and son.

Recently, an enemy of the prolific perennials appeared—Japanese beetles. At first, I enjoyed the beauty of their iridescent copper-colored shells. Later, I discovered the beetles dining upon the leaves of the climbing Concord grape vines, as well as the imprisoned raspberry plants. After mealtime, naught was left of the leaves but skeletons. My garden allies were under attack by a Japanese beetle air force. These insect miscreants spend their vitality flying about, eating and mating, an enviable lifestyle.

After conferring with my wife, "the Dish," commanding officer of our domestic unit, I loaded an AK-47 squirt gun with hose water and a dollop of dish detergent. I sprayed the invaders while they ate, which dulled their sheen and inhibited all of their pastimes. Our garden allies vehemently objected to the baptism in Dawn dish soap and demanded that General Dish convene a war council.

(I am proud to relate that after our three sons moved out on their own, we gave away our cats and our dog died, General Dish promoted me to the rank of Colonel, second in command of our household).

At our combat conclave, we fashioned a new strategy: use the beetle's best defense as our offense. The hexapods, when threatened, fold in their appendages and drop and roll, just as children learn as fire defense. While shaking an infested leaf, I held a canvas canister containing our soapy ammunition beneath. The startled beetles, their meal interrupted, folded, rolled and dropped into the bucket. In such a fashion, I have eliminated a small troop of privates and maybe a corporal or two. This approach is akin to removing a bucket of sand from the Sahara Desert. Our enemy commanders do not teach birth control in Dating Practices 101.

For our next assault, General Dish ordered that I purchase two Japanese beetle traps. As I was somewhat skeptical of their capability, I requested that we deploy but one. The device consists of an hourglass-shaped bag about 16 inches long, a plastic insert to hold it open, a hanger, and an attachable pheromone attractant. Hopefully, the enemy will sense the fragrance that intimates "hookers for free."

The wind was fresh and dispersed the alluring scent before I had the trap completed. Immediately, four beetles dove to their demise within the sex-scented sack of horrors. I set the trap, retreated, and watched in amazement as mating-crazed hopefuls flew in from parts unknown to join the orgy of death plunge.

With contrition, I asked permission to activate a second trap. I positioned the newest beetle brothel beneath our crab apple tree. Watch out, a swarm! Beetles, glistening beetles, six-legged beetles, beetles with spread wings and chewing mouth parts, and unbridled ardor emerged from the lilacs, the grass, the trees, from as far as the eye could see. I felt like an extra in a Japanese horror movie, *Attack of the Horny Hexapods,* with a soon-to-be-released unrated version, *Attack of the Copulating Coleopterans.*

The horde surged past me in such a wave that I was mere jetsam in its torrent. I fought for fresh air free from frantic, fertile, pheromone-following, ill-fated, flying fornicators. After my escape, I reflected, "The human race is not the most lustful species in creation, but many find the same fate."

Of the uncounted beetles, my two traps took in their fill. The remaining party goers circled the revelry like geeks at senior prom. The $9.98 expenditure for the traps was cheap retribution for my perennials and me even though a good share of the frenzied suitors did not find room at the inn.

For the price, I also acquired a life lesson: "Be wary of Chanel #5."

# # # # #

JEOPARDY

I'm saying it, as an all-American male, I have the right to watch the TV shows and movies of my choice without fear of placing myself in marital jeopardy. I'm sure that the Constitution would back me up.

The wife's gone for a while, shopping I suppose, although I'm not privy to her schedule or destinations. I'm prepping the recliner, closing the drapes, opening my preferred beverage and searching for the remote. I'm going to watch three R-rated action movies and an episode of *Breaking Bad*. Stallone, Schwarzenegger and Willis know how rack up the body count and Bryan Cranston is beyond despicable. I'm such a bad boy. And why shouldn't I be? That's what attracted her in the first place 44 years ago.

My mother, rest her soul, reveled in such theatrical mayhem. The wife finds little joy in such carnage, the volume necessary for peak enjoyment and my testosterone surge. She expresses her viewpoint in no uncertain terms. Yet she has no problem with viewing her barf bag shows when I'm in the room. Whoever said that men marry women akin to their mothers ought to be spiked.

I ask you, whose programs are the more offensive? Wifey enjoys the emergency room TV shows where a lame-brain walks in with a hunting arrow submerged in his head or some sorry soul in spelunking gear arrives skewered from shoulder to the hip socket by a stalactite. Equally disgusting is her show about prima donnas searching for the perfect wedding dress. Another of her abysmal programs exposes impoverished persons who have amassed a homestead of trash: magazines, bobble heads, sconces, appliances, assorted vehicles and years worth of take-out food containers, all accented by the occasional dead cat. A squad shows up adorned in coveralls and gasmasks to save the day, shovel out the hovel, and hold a garage sale.

I just answered my own question.

This bad boy is having a sip, while watching between his elevated feet, as Stallone wastes a platoon of North Vietnamese and Russian soldiers. Oh, bad word, the garage door is opening. She's home already. It's going to be a massacre. Where's the remote?

"Hi, dear. That was a short shopping trip. I hope you had fun. I'm taking in a few minutes of TV. Do you want to join me? It's couples week on *Jeopardy*."

# # # # #

CLARK

Rick talked to himself as he typed in the study, unknowingly within Cora's hearing; "Up to this point, my life has been characterized by a Clark Kent persona. That stops here and now. I'm superseding my tolerant facade with superlative strength of character. Laugh if you will, little wifey. I've compiled criticisms, complaints and comments, and I'm giving voice to the catalogue right now, in this writing."

From the living room, Cora commented, "Caution, Clark, compile, criticism, complaint, comment, and catalogue are just a few letters removed from compel, circumcision, compliant, committal, and catacomb."

- Rick is my name. Dick is not. Ricky is not.
- To all the *Dear Abby* clones—shut the hell up! While I'm at it, the same goes for Rush Limbaugh and that kid on the airplane.
- Our Norway maple tree is about 30 years old, 40 feet wide and 25 feet tall, much like the guy who sat next to me on the jet liner to Hawaii. "Exsqueeze me, yeah, that's right. I'm talking to you. Sit over there or buy two tickets or take the boat. Hey, that's my bag of peanuts."
- There should not be 87 shades of tan wall paint. Aren't any of you wall paint maker morons married?
- We had received half an inch of snow by the time I left work for home. On the way, I caught up to 27 cars and 11 semis driving bumper to bumper, side by side, at 6 mph, taking up every lane on the freeway. "Hey, nimrods, yeah, that's right. I'm talking to you. Learn to drive or stay home or make way. Get off your cell phones and pay attention… to this hand signal."

- After the snowfall, the plow displaced our downhill neighbor's snow drift and the road salt onto our yard and driveway. The snow will melt by April and the salt by June while I remain frosty.
- My uphill neighbor's unusable joints and cigarette butts turn up in my driveway, lawn and garage. "Hey, Mack, yeah, that's right. I'm talking to you. Stop smoking or buy a freaking ash tray or move to Swaziland."
- The McDonald's bathroom motion-activated appliances are either slow to react, empty, clogged or too powerful.
- The first sheet of McDonald's transparent teetotaler toilet tissue is impossible to find. "Hey, McDonalds, yeah, that's right. I'm talking to you. Don't you know the end result of a Big Mac, fries and a coke?"
- I've learned that:
    - When wrestling with my two-year-old grandson, he will mash my McNuggets.
    - Our loft railing is merely decorative.
    - Stain-resistant carpeting isn't stain-proof carpeting.
    - Water-resistant footwear isn't waterproof footwear.
    - Non-stick cookware is stick-resistant cookware.
    - Wood flooring should have a non-slip feature.
    - Rice in the salt shaker clogs the holes.
    - One baby generates more laundry than an entire household.
    - A new neighbor's toilet will clog after I've made a deposit.
    - Work-related special projects are assigned on Fridays.
    - My breakfast half grapefruit has better aim than Annie Oakley.
    - My Ozzy Osborne CD will stutter.

- My computer will stall at the best part of the video while producing some counter clockwise circling nonsense atop the arrested action.
- Without fail, the Wheaties will be soggy before they hit my mouth.
- The nightlight that is ineffective during the day will blind me at night.
- It takes $4 worth of charcoal to barbeque $4 worth of burger.
- While working in the forest, no matter how many layers of clothing I wear, a sticker will find its way into my jockey shorts.
- The tsp abbreviation on the liquid laxative label means teaspoon not tablespoon.

- Restaurant owners, if you want me to order a distinctive entrée, then turn up the freaking lights so I can read the menu. And print it in English without *italics*. And list the available side dishes on the same page, and, and, warn me if there is an up-charge for curly fries devoid of prostate-curdling spices.
- Waitresses, if you describe scrumptious desserts or point out a fancy table display without disclosing the prices, then expect your tip to pay for my selection.
- The uber-expensive songbird feed's advertisement made no mention of crows, grackles, starlings, several dozens of gray squirrels, raccoons and a lone turkey vulture, none of which so much as offered a single song for their supper.
- My hybrid, dwarf, acclimatized Haralson apple tree produced one apple last year. It broke the sapling and fell upon the ground. The gray squirrels ate it after they emptied my bird feeders.
- As far as I'm concerned, our DVR's primary responsibility is to record manly programs that are beyond Cora's sensibilities and my bedtime. Our DVR petered out two

minutes into *Busty Bikini Booty Babes from Space*. It has never failed to record *What not to Wear, Say Yes to the Dress, Extreme Home Makeover* or *American Idol*.

- Last summer a thunderstorm swept off my shingles and donated them to the neighborhood. The sun was shining next door at John's place. He was upset that one of my missiles knocked over his pitcher of margaritas.
- I called Verizon Wireless and blocked that 1-800-231-1000 phone number that has been computer dialing my cell phone incessantly. Today, I noted four calls from 1-800-231-1001.
- I urge that:
    - Cell phone owners refrain from texting while standing at the urinal.
    - Radio stations play more than three popular tunes per hour.
    - Dentists supply sunglasses or aim that freaking headlamp away from my eyes.
    - Medical doctors warm their hands and cool their attitude.
    - Calendars flip their own pages.
    - All wall-mounted pictures be hung level and properly centered.
    - Abstract painters offer a few words of explanation.
    - Poets offer a few words of explanation.
    - Women offer a few words of explanation.
    - Humanity bans the use of indoor tanning lotions.
    - Rappers learn to sing.
    - Politicians cease stating, "We need to...." Just take care of it.
    - Call-in-center trouble-shooters at least attempt to learn English.

- Music moguls choose any three music award programs and cancel the rest.
- Red carpet women, save all the fuss and just get naked.
- We have three outdoor thermometers. To get a sense of the temperature, I take an average of the readings. Meteorologists on TV, radio, and the Internet take an average and agree upon a forecast.
- Americans of Chinese ancestry; do your kids a favor. Stop naming them Hu, Hung, Lo, Ho, Dung, Dong, Wang, Fu, or combinations thereof.
- How many women's magazines does one woman need?
- A humble prayer: Oh please God, place the following English words and phrases on a 20-year moratorium. You may reinstate them after my ascension: annoying, basically, amazing, decadent, athleticism, really, seriously, disturbing, no, as well, it's like, and just for the heck of it, add fart to the list. Amen. Whatever.
- I only want one Kleenex at a time from the box!
- I saved soda cans for cash recycling. The nearest redemption center is in Biloxi.
- Lyricists, find another job if you can't do better than *whoa o whoa o whoa, la la la la la* or *baby baby baby*.
- How many ways can a person get CSIed?
- I wonder why ...
  - All credit card bills are due on the same day.
  - With all the ads featuring plump, red-cheeked, smiling babies, the purported research, and the $18.99 per box price tag, baby deposits continually escape their diapers.
  - Two or more major appliances expire within one pay check period.
  - *Wet Wipes* need to be unscented or non-allergenic.

- I've not been able to create those contrasting lawn stripes when I cut the grass.
- The newspaper, when folded, always wrinkles the article I'm reading.
- *The War Between the States* needs to be reenacted.
- My 1,200-page dictionary doesn't list the word proactive.
- My thesaurus doesn't list synonyms for perspicacious.
- Every pair of size 36"x32" jeans I buy fits differently.

- Nine times out of ten the Country Crock Spread slips off of my butter knife.
- I stopped on the way home from work and bought five 24-oz. loaves of white bread. At 5:30 a.m. the next morning, I spooned up some Country Crock. The bread bag was empty save heels and crumbs.
- How much additional chocolate does it take for a cake to be extra chocolaty, fudgy, decadent, or German?
- I have not yet been able to enjoy soda with noticeable fizz from the last liter of a two liter bottle.
- I don't eat foods unless I can see what's inside them. Some examples: Mexican dishes, hors d'oeuvres, cabbage rolls, jelly donuts, and Brussels sprouts.
- I don't eat food dishes with "surprise" in the title.
- I don't eat foods with names like leek soup, shitake gravy, or anise candy.
- Our recliner has a gap between the upright and the seat where my wallet, comb, pocket knife, coins, pen, butt cheeks, buttons, popcorn, candy and pizza choose to reside. The foot rest is too short and its ten comfort settings are missing the correct one. The down-filled head hump kinks my neck. Fits Cora to a tee, though.

- I've recently opened a Facebook account and friended Cora. She didn't reply. I activated her account, accepted my request and wrote a seductive letter to me. I bet my seven friends are envious.
- The bed covers end up on the Cora's side and her cold feet on my side.
- Here in the U.S.A, most people have mixed ancestral heritage that has over time smoothed out inherent idiosyncrasies. Cora is full-blooded Norwegian.

Cora startled Rick while stealthily reading over his shoulder. As he lunged to close his laptop, she gibed, "How's that superlative strength of character working out for you, *Clark?*"

# # # # #

CABLE SERVICES FOR FREE

I called our cable service provider today, just on a whim. After a Spanish-language bypass, several instructed number selections, the maximum waiting period, and a warning of potential clandestine monitoring, a foreign national joined the call.

"Hello, thith is Fartinand De Marco Abpoo. How may I help you?"

"Hi, I am Rick Wehler. My phone number is ……….. Do you have any movie channel specials currently available?"

As cable services are expensive, clipping the company for a few bucks now and again gratifies the frugal genes I inherited from my Scottish ancestors.

Mr. Abpoo replied, "Why, yeth, Mithter Dick. May I call you Mithter Dick?"

I responded in kind, "Why, sure, Mr. Fart, but I would prefer to be called Mister Rick."

Mr. Abpoo comforted, "Yeth, thomtimes the phone lines between the U.Th. and India cause mithprounthiations. Jutht let me check your account for a minute please."

Upon his return, I noted a change in the cable representative's attitude as he exclaimed, "Wow, Mithter Dick, you have a large package!"

"Mr. Fart, how do you know that all the way from India?" I queried.

He answered, "That thatithtic is lithted on your account."

I mumbled, "You folks have way too much information."

Mr. Abpoo's enthusiasm peaked, "Yeth, Mr. Dick, as a result of your large package, you can have the HBO and

Thinemax movie channels free for a year, jutht to try them out!"

I replied with equal enthusiasm, "Great, Mr. Fart, old buddy, sign me up!"

Mr. Abpoo concluded our conversation by saying, "Your new thervithes should be active within 5 minuth. Please call uth any time 24/theven for athithtanth."

After two return calls to cable thervices, stop that, services, to request that both of my televisions be programmed properly with all the proffered channels, the flat screen excitement could begin.

I am now freely funded and fully able to avoid watching all of the deplorable HBO award-winning series such as *The Wire, the Sopranos, Six Feet Under*, and *The Cat House*. At least I don't have to pay for not watching them.

Perhaps after *the Hookers on the Point* season finale, HBO will present a 24-hour Disney classic cartoon marathon. I could watch *Lady and the Tramp* a dozen times and never tire of deciphering the arcane meanings of sharing a meatball or the accidental kiss in the middle of a spaghetti strand. This movie assuredly has a rat in the baby's room.

Or I could view *Snow White and the Seven Dwarfs*. It has been my private practice to emulate the pandering foibles of Dopey, Happy, and Bashful. I do not though identify as readily with the other Dwarfs.

Doc, no way, I am afraid of Docs. Sneezy sought therapy, dosed with Claritin and lost his identity.

Sleepy must not know about the effects of complex sugars and Grumpy needs a high colonic.

There you go. I understand the Seven Dwarfs better than I do our nation's coterie of Supreme Court Justices. That's ok. The Dwarfs have more relevance in my life.

CABLE SERVICES FOR FREE

After 10 p.m., the Cinemax channels offer a dazzling array of slasher and soft-core porn movies. By that time, all legitimate god-fearing children are fast asleep and in no danger of acquiring socially relevant practices.

As my recent psych evaluation showed my emotional age to be that of a high-end adolescent, I am also asleep by 10 p.m. dreaming my own Cinemax facsimiles. Once again, I don't have to pay.

I hope that the cable company will forgive my failure to improve their movie channel's ratings, as on Monday I plan to negotiate with them concerning DVR and On Demand services. If successful, I will be able to record all the shows I don't watch, anytime I want, for free.

# # # # #

FRESH AIR

Between a ragged arbor vitae hedge and a string of weathered one-stall garages stood a stout, elderly man staring wistfully from beneath a tattered ball cap into the distant sky. His fancifully priced garage sale mementoes were failing to tempt his infrequent shoppers and, as I approached, he chuckled in a self-deprecating fashion. Ripples undulated between his burdened beltline and the rangy tufts of white hair escaping the neckline of his faded, under-sized tank shirt.

"Yes sir, fine day, yup. I was thinking that no one else would bother stopping by. This one-cup coffee maker (*patting the coffee maker*), I paid $93 for it and 10 bucks each for those two boxes of coffee inserts. It makes that fancy kind a coffee. You know—the ones with nutty flavors, spices and such. You put the insert in under this flap and pour the water in here. My wife doesn't care much for it anymore since she lost so much weight. I'd like to get $50 for it. I'll throw in those two packages of coffee inserts for free. Hang on just a minute. I got a phone call."

"Yes, this is Melvin Smathers. Well, I called earlier because my DVR box doesn't work. I laid out $29.99 to have it installed. Yeah, I'll hold on."

"Sure, have a look, some mighty nice clothes my wife used to wear before she lost so much weight. That blouse is pure silk. It cost $123 and change. I'd like to get $50 for it. I'll throw in that matching pair of pants. I don't think she wants to see 'em anymore."

"No, I wasn't talking to you. I'm doing two things at once here. I could go to Dish Network or Satellite TV, you know.

You should swap out that box and give back my installation fee. Yeah, I'll hold while you check on that."

"It sure is a busy street today with that auction sale at the house down on the corner. I heard some old guy lived there. He didn't get out much. His kids moved him to a nursing home. and they're selling off his memories. You'd think I'd get a bit of overflow traffic. Maybe I should put up a bigger sign."

"My wife's inside getting ready for something. She stays pretty busy since she lost so much weight. I thought I'd come outside and get some fresh air. Maybe sell some of this stuff. It doesn't get used anyhow."

"I paid six hundred dollars to Ducks Unlimited for this stuffed teal drake and his glass display table (*pats the table*). He sits inside, sort of watching over things. Maybe he's a wood duck. I still like him a lot, but the wife's lost weight and goes out a lot now, so I got to get rid of some of this stuff."

"No, I wasn't talking to you. The last 4 digits of my social security number are 6004."

"Think I'll close up shop and check out that auction, even though it's probably just overpriced personal stuff. Not many customers stopping by here anyhow. I heard the old guy sat inside all day. His kids moved him to a nursing home. Don't much care for sitting inside looking out the windows like that duck (*points at the duck*). We both need some fresh air."

"A hundred dollars? Why it cost more than a hundred dollars just to get that darned duck stuffed! I paid six hundred dollars to Ducks Unlimited for him (*arms crossing*). Couldn't take less than $175. See how he's sitting in the marsh weeds just taking things in? "

"I grew up on a farm in northern Minnesota, plenty of fresh air (*both arms spreading wide while drawing a deep breath*). It wasn't so much a farm as it was a swamp. Looking back, we were mighty poor, but didn't much know it. There were so many ducks swimming in the marsh, taking off and landing, going wherever they pleased. We didn't shoot 'em, just watched."

"I wanted to fly away too and find a life of my own. Took Jenny from her parent's place, got married and headed to the cities. I did some welding, small engine repair and the like back when such was needed. Never hurt for work. All six kids are out there now (*sweeping right arm gesture*). See 'em on occasion. Don't like sitting in that apartment; got to get some fresh air."

"You know, I paid six hundred dollars to Ducks Unlimited for that caged duck (*head nodding towards the duck*). It's a teal or maybe a wood duck. Couldn't take less than $150 for him."

FRESH AIR

"So your nephew likes ducks, does he? Yeah, I remember hundreds of 'em on the farm coming and going just as they pleased. I can see 'em (*staring into the distant sky*) just plain as day. Well, a change of scenery might do him some good. Let's say, maybe, $125."

"Don't much care for being caged up in that apartment." (*Thumb pointing back over his right shoulder*).

"You only have $117, huh? Well, ok, he isn't going to be flying away any time soon either, so I suppose it doesn't matter much. Got to get some fresh air. Think I'll walk down to that old guy's auction. Fresh air and exercise are good for ya; live longer, lose weight. You ever saw a fat duck?"

"No, lady, I wasn't talking to you."

# # # # #

TICK AND DICK

I have a story to tell about a close personal friend who will remain anonymous. He much enjoys forestry work at the 65-acre woodland retreat, Westwoods. Although an excellent hobby, it's not without its hazards.

On a recent visit while clearing invasive plants from around the base of a dead elm tree, this self-ascribed formidable forester spotted a morel mushroom. Believing that where there was one there must be another, he got down on hands and knees, and for the next hour or so, crawled around overturning dead bark, fallen leaves and skeletal remains. All the while he disturbed the rank and file of indigenous and somewhat resentful insect life.

After a harvest of 24 morels, which are well loved by his soon-to-be-estranged wife, the famed forester resumed his earlier endeavors. At day's end, as was his practice, he removed his soiled and infested clothing, deposited same within a laundry bag, and donned clean apparel before driving home to reunite with his devoted spouse.

Upon home coming, the fastidious forester removed his clean clothes and, for safety's sake, deposited them in the previously mentioned laundry bag as well. By so doing, he had hoped to confine any insects that may have hitchhiked to his home with him.

The warmhearted woodsman then bathed and performed a personal inspection for creeping commuters. Mrs. Forester, having been raised in a log cabin, did not care for multi-legged creatures, claiming that to this day they still make her skin crawl. She denied the friendly forester greetings of any sort until all signs of forest contamination had been extirpated.

TICK AND DICK

The weathered woodsman's aged body parts required frequent restroom visits, an affliction which that evening proved to be of value. While so engaged, he encountered a black, twitching tick the size of a hermit crab firmly fastened to his... um, well... private part as it gained sustenance through its intricate IV system.

Rather than resort to gross entomological and physiological terminology, I'll just bestow a nickname upon each of the combatants. The frightened forester latched onto Tick with his trusty pliers. Doesn't everyone have such a tool in their medicine cabinet?

Thus began a tug of war between Tick and Dick that stretched both to the lengths of their endurance. The freaked forester offered his entire lexicon of sundry expletives on Tick's behalf. Much to the relief of the worried woodsman, Dick broke free but not without relinquishing the chunk to which Tick was so attached.

The wounded woodsman yelped like a stepped-on puppy. Tick, although victorious in some sense, completed several swirls about the bowl before the final flush sent it toward the Hereafter to be reincarnated as a payday loan officer or an auto mechanic.

The wife of the wobbly woodsman wanted an explanation for the other-worldly wail and the spate of blasphemies bawled from behind closed doors. The flustered forester justified his outbursts as best he could by placing sole blame upon the recently deceased Tick.

Mrs. Forester, after several indescribable facial expressions, eeuwwes and insensitive giggles, commanded that Dick remain far from her company, zipped within its own penal prison until further notice. The woebegone woodsman hoped that luck would grant Dick a conjugal visit soon after the conclusion of the forestry season. Knock on wood.

El Diablo

My parents purchased our first house in 1958. It was a small rambler, the second dwelling in a housing development entitled Woodland Hills, due to its lack of both and the swamp. The same humorist dubbed a rutted dirt path in front of our home, Birch Road, yes—no birch trees, and christened the swamp Lake Charlotte.

Lake Charlotte shared surplus swamp water with our septic tank, which in turn shared its endowment with my basement living quarters. Following innumerable payments to the local honey dipper consortium, Smitty's Septic Service, Dad purchased his own portable septic pump. After lights out, Dad, at times, with my reluctant assistance, used the pump to return the septic tank's enriched swamp water to the bog.

In the course of time, when Woodland Hills was overflowing with other homeowners, fate blessed Dad with a backdoor neighbor in possession of a big, black, devil dog, El Diablo. Nightly it awoke the neighborhood with relentless, vindictive barking as if it voiced a horror movie sound track.

From the hellhound's habitation located along our shared back fence line, El Diablo reveled in its ability to summon Dad's inner demons. Dad phoned the beast's owners at the commencement of each recital and invited their audience. With his overtures declined and the certainty of future performances, Dad came up with a scheme.

While celebrating the rite of the septic tank, Dad diverted the effluent's path from the swamp to our neighbor's backyard by snaking the hose through a portal in the back fence, avoiding Lucifer's lair. Dad laughed until he cried and howled in concert with the pump's drone and El Diablo's harangue. He came to relish the trio's engagements. Until the advent of city water and sewer, Dad's backdoor recipients boasted the most luxuriant lawn in the neighborhood.

An Innocent Bet

My sixteen-year-old, pale blue eyes proclaimed innocence as effectively as would a public notice emblazoned upon my tattered baseball hat. Such evident naiveté belied my inherent business acumen. Opportunities to showcase this innate ability began at the age of ten with the birth of my sister, Sandi.

Our parents worked a couple evenings per week, a circumstance that required my 8½-year old sister, Rhonda, and I to watch over our family's newest acquisition. Some folks work during their retirement as unpaid volunteers. I was neither retired nor volunteering, only unpaid.

Rumors of an excellent boy babysitter invading the sanctity of girl's work spread quickly in our new community. Within weeks, I began earning significant amounts of legal tender by riding herd on nearly every neighborhood kid between the ages of two weeks and eight years.

Babysitting was lucrative employment for the early 1960s with a tax-free cash wage of twenty-five cents per hour. After the obligatory savings account deposit, 50 percent of reported earnings, as required by my fatherly financial adviser, I had enough cash remaining to buy all the malted milk balls I could pound down. I used my sugar-fueled energy to advantage and worked hours far beyond those allowed by child labor laws.

The kids enjoyed my strange sense of humor, another hereditary gift that lives on in infamy to this day. A further endowment was the ability to adapt my emotional age to that of my charges. That empathy as yet abides, but it hit the glass ceiling at high end adolescence according to modern psych tests.

At today's age of 58, my teenage passions are at times at odds with my contemporaries, but let those folks suffer as they may.

Daytime babysitting was soon replaced by sod installation, lawn mowing, weed eradication, and creature removal. These appointments paid upwards of $1 per hour depending on the length of the snake. As I reached the advanced age of 16, I was no longer satisfied with my financial success, especially when my friend Bruce informed me of a job opening in the produce department at Don Wright Supervalu.

After school, I hitched a ride on Bruce's school bus that stopped nearby the store. There I filled out my first employment application. It requested an itemization of previous business experience. Mike, the grocery store assistant manager, wasn't impressed by my listing.

Even so, the next afternoon, Mike placed a call to our home. Mother, our family's answering machine and monitoring service, understanding the call's urgency, summoned me from my other endeavors to the kitchen phone, acting as if there was another phone somewhere else in the house. Mike offered me the job and asked that I show up at the store, now. Having nearly consumed my latest acquisition of malt balls, I yelled, "Mom, I got a job."

Mom replied patiently, "RICKY, DON'T SCREAM INTO THE PHONE!"

As a matter of record, my name is Rick.

Mom loaned me her well-used Volkswagen Beetle and I drove my innocent frame of mind, without the baseball hat, five miles to the store. Mike introduced me to Marv, the produce manager and my new boss. Marv's attitude affirmed his mid-twenties age as did his brown, jelly-roll haircut and the cigar stub jammed into the corner of his mouth.

Marv took a full sixty seconds to assign my first task: place the contents of twenty cases of grapefruit into bags of six each. He then left via the back door for his girlfriend's home, certainly laughing all the way there, knowing that the bags would normally hold five grapefruit.

As I forcefully removed the lid from the first box, a green powdery substance followed the box top as the tail of a comet. Through the air arched a beautiful, living, mono-chromatic, spring-green, molded rainbow. I had to wipe clean every single grapefruit. In the absence of proper supplies, my new apron did the job, outlining itself nicely with enough green flora organisms to infuse every uncovered fiber of my one and only white business shirt. By the end of my first shift, my entire personage was a living, breathing community of penicillin-producing parasites.

Marv found my innocence refreshing. He was, indeed, expectant of continued opportunities for practical jokes and various forms of hazing. Such entertainment was third only to women and gambling. Marv pursued any female not currently receiving social security and then wagered on his purported success. I was the perfect comedic relief to his stressful avocations.

Marv's bookie called every Monday at 4 p.m. If Marv's sure-thing let him down, then he'd assign me to answer the phone and divert the bookie's call to the following Monday. One glorious afternoon, Marv sauntered into our work area paging through a newspaper. (I wasn't aware that Marv read anything without a centerfold.) With a cigar-laden, self-satisfied smile, he pointed to a small article about a local bookie who had been nabbed by the police, thanks to an anonymous tip.

My parents had warned me about girls and gambling, but not about Marv. I, therefore, had a strong fear of Marv's chosen pleasures and was totally naive concerning Marv. I had been saving 50 percent of my earnings for six years and was not interested in risking any part of my stash on chancy pursuits like girls or gambling. The only girls I couldn't avoid were relatives. The only bets I had been part of were rhetorical when a bully at school would say, "Wanna bet how many times I can pound you before the bell rings?"

Marv asked, "Do you wanna bet that I can tell you exactly which store phone calls will be for me, a quarter per call?" Dad forbad gambling of any kind, but insisted that I obey authority, particularly his own. What was I to do? I had lost $1.25, one hour's wage, before I discovered that Marv was calling himself by dialing from line one to line two. Marv also insisted on arm wrestling me for a $1.25 bet. Marv's swift victory seeded an idea within me that would turn my lost wages into a shrewd investment.

II

My friend Harry and his family moved in across the street. He and I made a great David and Goliath team. I towered about 5 foot 6 when cheating just a bit and weighed 134 lbs. after supper. Harry reached 6 feet tall with his knees bent and weighed 205 lbs. in his gym shorts. He wrestled, lifted weights, ran daily, and didn't own a neck.

Meanwhile, Marv was raking in the cash by trouncing every sucker in the store at arm wrestling. He bragged incessantly. The idea seeded after my previous loss burst forth. It was time to set Marv up. I challenged him in front of his current girlfriend: "Marv, you aren't so tough just because you can beat a few high school kids. I bet you can't beat every high school kid."

Marv removed his cigar and replied, "Wanna bet? You little turd (word substitution), you think you're so smart. I bet you five bucks that I can beat any friend you have."

I tightened the noose by saying, "Five bucks! That's a whole day's pay. Are you nuts?"

Marv countered, "Hey, you're the one who started this. Now put up or shut up."

I meekly gave into the bet by puling, "Ok, ok, I bet you five bucks that my friend Harry can beat you."

We set up the contest date and location as Friday after school at the store. I hired Harry for 10 percent of the expected winnings.

Surprisingly, Marv didn't brag about the upcoming match. Friday afternoon, I pointed out his opponent. Marv watched as Harry lumbered down the produce aisle towards the backroom. Harry's thighs rubbed together all the way to his knees. His upper arms had a similar problem with his chest. Marv removed his cigar stump, tried in vain to display a confident smile and gulped.

Harry gave Marv a head-to-toe once over and merely grunted. Their elbows were on the bench and Marv's arm was pinned before he could blink. Harry left without comment. I collected my five bucks and set aside Harry's share of the winnings, fifty cents.

In a split second, I'd recovered all of my gambling losses with a two-dollar surplus. I invested a dollar of the winnings into Marv's football pool and won another ten dollars.

Later, I bragged to Dad about how I had set up Marv. Dad scowled and said, "Do you want to bet who'll be pumping out the septic tank tonight?"

# # # # #

A Dish of Norwegian Crow

Cora Sue Johnson and I began dating in June of 1970. She was an 18-year-old knockout Norwegian country girl with a high school diploma. I was a 20-year-old average Joe, city boy, college student. Despite my age, I had little experience with successful dating. I vowed, henceforth, to be myself: studious, fun-loving, and strong-willed even if I had to eat crow on occasion.

I called Cora, whom I was soon to nickname "Dish," and asked her out on a date to go target shooting at the Minnesota River, not far from Shakopee. I enjoyed firing my Browning semi-automatic .22 rifle, and crowing now and then about my marksmanship.

Cora Sue Johnson, 1970.

We arrived at a secluded spot along the river, sat upon the bank and waited for whatever flotsam happened by. I took aim at a reasonably sized stick drifting with the current about ten yards offshore and let loose. My third shot hit the stick and my fifth shot splintered it. I looked over at Cora with unabashed pride.

I handed the Browning to Cora and commenced with the following instructions. "Pull the magazine rod out of the rear of the stock, load the .22 shells, lead first, into the stock's side slot. Replace the rod and press the stock up against your shoulder. Look down the barrel and position the sight at the front of the barrel within the V at the back. Place your target on top of the sight. Are you all set?"

She replied in the affirmative.

I then instructed, "Cock the rifle, which will load a shell into the chamber. Grab a deep breath and let it out slowly. Take aim at your mark, and squeeze the trigger gently." Man, was I on target with this woman.

Cora spotted a small stick about thirty yards from shore. I asked her to point it out as I couldn't see it. She made ready and fired all 12 shots in a flash. The stick split and took flight with her first shot as did the ensuing remnants with each succeeding round. I can't say for sure that every shot found its mark as the target was small, far away, and it all happened so fast.

> The river laughed and Cora smiled
> As she returned the smoking gun to her beau.
> I tried to save face while I deservedly dined
> On a dish of Norwegian crow.

# # # # #

Afterthoughts

Cora always opened the exit doors for me when we paid a visit to her small Northern Minnesota hometown. I finally asked her why she did so. She replied, "This is hunting territory. The first one through the door usually gets the bullet."

#

I visited a garage sale that offered baby clothes, vintage *Playboy* magazines and .22 shells. If I had a baby or bought a *Playboy* magazine, then Cora would find use for the .22 shells.

#

She loves me, she loves me not, she loves me. I'm stopping there.

#

When we were newly married, I was in charge of everything. A few years back, I figured out that I'm in charge of nothing. I don't know how that happened.

#

Lunch TMI

Peanut butter and jelly sandwiches have been the mainstay of my lunch time menu since I became a Gerber graduate and they'll remain so until I'm once again required to dine upon baby food. I've yet to find my midday meal mundane because PBJ recipes are as limitless and imaginative as a diva's wardrobe.

In order to defend both my penchant for PBJ sandwiches and my assortment assertion, I'll dig into my favorite ingredients beginning with the peanut butter. There exists a myriad of peanut butter brands and blends that contribute to my culinary compulsion such as Skippy, Jiff, Planters, and creamy, chunky and natural. No doubt George Washington Carver would be pleased. Skippy Creamy has replaced Skippy Chunky as my preferred variety. (My former favorite chose to harass my ever-increasing landscape of gum tissue.)

The second category of ingredients, jelly, is even more diverse than peanut butter. There's a jelly for nearly every fruit that's grown and probably a few veggie jellies as well. My favorite, though, is grape jelly. I do indulge in apple, blueberry, cherry, plum, rhubarb, and strawberry, to name a few. However, I avoid others such as orange marmalade and raspberry jam. Those miscreants contain hunks of rind or indigestible seeds that imbed themselves within my most secluded dental sanctuaries. The infiltrators evade waxed dental floss, sonic tooth brushes, water picks, dental hygienists, and MRI scans.

While a youth, my parents' budget allowed for little more than white bread. As a man of independent means, I've branched out into other breads for my peanut butter and jelly concoctions such as French, Vienna, rye, pumpernickel, and hamburger and hotdog buns. I refuse, though, to dine upon doctor-recommended, whole-grain breads with their nutritional chunks of debris for the reasons previously noted.

I may be in the minority believing that whatever bread I choose should, at first, be spread with butter, not a lavish amount, just enough to keep the jelly from soaking though but not so much as to encourage it to slide out. I'm told that if I'm on a physical fitness kick, then I should switch to margarine, but that is not for me. Most brands contain heart-healthy vegetable oils, trans-fats and yellow dies instead of unwholesome butter fat. (I misspelled dyes on purpose.)

Every now and then I'll add tasty tidbits to my PBJ sandwich, such as banana slices, mini-marshmallows, chocolate chips, frosting sprinkles, or graham cracker and vanilla wafer pieces.

For fun, I'll fashion my PBJ sandwich on square bread and cut it in half diagonally rather than horizontally. In that way, the halves form two cool right triangles instead of two passé rectangles. Each half then sports three corners instead of four and an expanded crust-free soft eating surface along the hypotenuse. Occasionally, I'll slice a square sandwich into five fillets that I've named fingers and manicure the crusts.

Years ago, I invented a second sandwich slicing system, which turned out to be popular with the little mouths of our children and the big mouth of our nosy neighbor, who just happened to be the president of a local gossip organization, the Welcome Wagon.

I prepared a PBJ finger sandwich for her unexpected visit, cut each finger into three segments, named it a knuckle sandwich and offered her one. I nearly burst an artery suppressing my laughter when a glob of grape jelly fell into her pumped-up, Wonder-bra cleavage. Cora's glare encouraged me to leave the room.

Lunch TMI

As I surreptitiously glanced back over my shoulder, I witnessed madam politely recover the grape glob with her napkin. I'm sure she could've slurped it up with her prehensile tongue.

If you add to my PBJ favorites all of the other varieties of peanut butter, jelly, bread, butter, butter facsimiles, tasty tidbits, and slicing styles, then the sum total of PBJ sandwiches bests the side effects count of a typical prescription drug.

When my baby sister, Ru, and I were aged in the single digits and times were particularly tough, Mom replaced our pricey peanut butter and jelly sandwiches with brown sugar sandwiches. Each consisted of two slices of white bread spread with oleo, a substance that looked like lard. The artificially colored yellow oleo that resembled butter was illegal in our home state of Minnesota.

Mom stuck the bread slices together on three sides, thanks to the greasy oleo. She then poured brown sugar into the pockets, pressed them shut, wrapped the sandwiches in wax paper, placed them into our lunch bags and offered a silent prayer. I liked the way the brown sugar clumped up by lunch time.

One morning, Dad subbed for Mom and made the brown sugar sandwiches to her specifications. Not long thereafter, he and three accomplices drove to Iowa and smuggled back several bricks of yellow oleo.

In the 1950s, no one suspected a correlation between complex sugars and hyperactivity. Rhonda and I were part of an elite group of grade-school children plagued by the yet-to-be-diagnosed, sugar-induced attention deficit disorder. We were unable to sit still, focus, keep quiet, or speak intelligibly. (That hasn't changed much in my case.)

My second-grade teacher, Miss Magimpsi, had little patience for post-lunch-time shenanigans. She frequently raised my classroom standing by lifting me out of my desk chair via my left ear while employing her entire lexicon of profane euphemisms such as "chrimany," "the sainted mother," and "you little doody." Little doody always made me laugh, which didn't help my ear much.

Mom couldn't understand my teacher's continual complaints. By the time I'd been excused and walked the mile home from school, my sugar buzz had worn off. I was depressed and lethargic. Mom, fearing my mood swings, activated an accepted mid-century, cure all—a belly-busting enema. I can't count, nor do I care to remember, the number of times I lay face down in the bathtub hiding my eyes from the reddish-brown rubbery bottle with its snaking hose that Mom slung from the tub's towel dowel. To this day the sight of any comparable container puckers me up like a lemon-fed chipmunk.

Once in a while, Dad prepared our school lunches, when Mom needed some private time to contemplate the teacher's notes. Dad was imaginative when it came to sandwiches. He called his inventions "Fistarus sandwiches." One exceptional example comes to mind. Dad made it from expensive ingredients: two pieces of Wonder Bread (a real treat because Captain Kangaroo and Mr. Green Jeans both said that it was the best bread anywhere), mayonnaise instead of oleo, liverwurst, and sweet pickle chips. I could hardly wait for lunch time.

Dad served untold other Fistarus creations, although their makeup escapes me at the moment. When he was in control of our lunches, I was able to escape the effects of brown sugar sandwiches: hyperactivity, ear lengthening, nasty notes, mood swings, and colon cleansings.

To her credit, one of Mom's evening meals leaned towards the unusual. Dad referred to it as a Fistarus meat loaf. It contained all the week's leftovers—animal, vegetable, and mineral—mixed together and cranked through the meat grinder. She baked the conglomerate in a cake pan and we swamped the final product in catsup.

Well, I've gotten off subject, lost my sense of time, and missed the lunch hour. No matter, we're out of peanut butter.

#####

PREAMBLE

An overpowering sugar buzz kindled a two-hour writing frenzy, during which I recorded the first draft of "A Singular Leather Jacket." As per normal, I asked my wife, Cora the Dish, to read the story and offer her comments, knowing full well that the final product would be dozens of rewrites later.

Continuing in habit, I printed my rough drafts and reviewed their word order, vocabulary, and flights of fancy. Somehow, editing a story impressed upon printer paper provides better results than revising my ramblings while displayed upon a computer monitor.

After I printed a copy of the nearly complete "A Singular Leather Jacket," I embarked upon a divergent strategy for this debutante's cotillion. I cut back on complex carbohydrates for the night and sequestered my virginal anecdote in hopes that it or I might mature during the allotted overnight hours.

The following morning, I replaced several obscure words except for neologisms, eliminated neologisms except for thriftmanship, and, painstakingly preserved each and every flight of fancy and considered the work complete.

A SINGULAR LEATHER JACKET

I recently learned that my mother's maternal grandfather, my mother's mother's father, was a Scotsman, rather than an Englishman as I had supposed. One might expect such a misunderstanding, as "Jonesy" was oft times referred to by his profession as an English sea captain. In actuality, the only English part of him was the ship he commanded.

A Singular Leather Jacket

Great-Grandpa's journeys took him to far off lands such as Argentina, where he courted and married a native maiden. I, therefore, incorrectly surmised that I had an Argentinean great-grandmother. Great-Grandma Del Conto proved to be a Chilean immigrant. Although my Hispanic lineage may be of interest, my intent here is to highlight my Scottish ancestry.

(You may have noted that I employed the descriptors, my mother's maternal grandfather plus my mother's mother's father. The additional delineation afforded me a modicum of payback to the computer's auto-correct feature that is currently suffering arrhythmia. A while back, I emailed my wife, "I plan an evening meeting at Burdella's. It will be exhausting. Don't wait up." The auto-correct altered "at Burdella's" to read, at the Bordello. The marriage counselor was unsympathetic.)

I discovered two additional Scottish ancestors when I learned my mother's middle name was Bruce. The purpose of her unconventional masculine moniker was to preserve her fraternal grandparents' Scottish legacy as members of the Clan Bruce.

In hopes of reckoning my total percentage of Scotsman blood, I awakened my 1960s college calculator, a tri-talented slide rule, that at one time was the unchallenged master of trigonometry, calculus, and chemistry. Together we ciphered that with three Scottish great-grandparents, I am 37.5 percent Scotsman. If I consider my father's lifelong occupation, salesman, rather than his ancestry, and add together his 50 percent contribution to my life force with my 37.5 percent maternal Scottish legacy, I should then be able to boast a sum total of 87.5 percent inherent thriftsmanship. This heritage explains my frugal fervor and such behaviors as garage sale shopping, for which I have become somewhat famous in my own estimation.

During the warm seasons, our city's residents stage garage sales. Rather than trust my memory to quote the garage sale description from another story, please allow me to cut and paste it here.

> "*By local definition, it makes no difference if the sale is held in the garage, basement, living room, yard or tree house. It is still a garage sale. The proprietors sell treasures that have lost their charm, clothing that no longer fits or has more than the legally allowed stained surface area, furnishings that retain most of their legs and cushions, and items from every room and closet that can be personally autographed in the dust that masks their identity.*"

While prospecting Thursday's garage sales, I discovered a goldmine. Ahem, based upon the prices I paid the proprietor, I might claim tin mine as a better descriptor. My first acquisition, twelve t-shirts that boasted the coveted Nike label and their original price tags, was a true Scotsman dickered-down-deal when the agent accepted my offer of $8 for the collection. It's uncommon to find clothing of such quality in my size, as few manufacturers in the Southeast Asian countries understand the combined effects of weight lifting and milkshakes.

At this selfsame sale, I sighted several pairs of perfectly sized blue jeans. Time out—I don't understand why one piece of clothing, in this case a pair of blue jeans, is called a pair, when in reality it is not twins, or why one example is named in the plural, jeans. The sign stated that six pairs of jeans were for sale, which should indicate at least twelve of them.

Another example of preposterous apparel plurals, if you please, is the feminine undergarment "panties." Although I claim but little expertise in any particulars concerning women or their attire, I feel justified in stating that most of their gender would avoid the purchase of two or more of the same style or color of any garment including underwear. So why use a plural for a singular?

Herein is another conundrum. After 39 years of marriage, style and color remain non-issues when I'm granted the privilege to ogle modeled panties. Why all the fuss? Who else is going to see it, them? I own about a dozen tidy whities that provide the needed service. I cannot distinguish one from the other.

As our household's designated laundry maven, I have learned after a few unintended errors, to air dry fashionable feminine panties rather than machine dry them. This proven method prevents the gossamer lingerie from passing through the dryer's lint filter, exiting its exhaust port, and drifting upon a whiff of wind as a feather.

Back to my point, one pair of panties should equal two sets. No, that's not right. Do three pairs of panties equal two-to-the-third-power panties? Such a mystery is nearly as mind numbing as the current effects of retrograde time travel conjectured by sci-fi authors.

Thanks to their scientific imaginings, I now feel it reasonable to surmise that the unusual benefactor of men's clothing at this garage sale, who happens to be just my size, is in fact a future me who had traveled back in time and was marooned there. So there was I, older than now, my possessions for sale, and dead besides. How unfortunate, in that he, as me, was one of the few who shared my measurements. With but only an estimated dozen or so of us peculiar consumers nationally, I promptly purchased all six pairs of blue jeans on sale at his, my, our, garage sale without haggling the 50 cent per pair price.

Without apology, I admit to a predilection toward leather jackets of all varieties. I do become chilled on occasion, but if I were to wear all of my jacket purchases at the same moment, I would certainly expire from the weight of my foolishness. Out on the driveway, on a sagging pipe propped twixt two step ladders, hung the finest leather jacket I have ever witnessed as an offering at a garage sale. May I say that I have seen plenty, and I own most of them. An evident time-travel paradox, even in death, I would not have offered this singular leather jacket for sale to the dickering dolts who frequent garage sales. Perhaps I planned to sell it to me. There it was hidden amongst several XXL floral bedizened senior lady garments, a couple of infant snowsuits and I swear that other item was a zoot suit.

I reached for the leather jacket, hoping that none of the other shopping contenders had spotted it. The weak-willed, dilapidated hanger upon which my jacket was displayed bowed at a precipitous angle. The jacket laughed heartily through its elongated, metal, multi-toothed grill as I attempted to lift it from its current residence. It dragged me to the concrete and spewed forth insults such as "what a girl" and "maybe your wife should lift me" mocked at such volume as to attract the gaze of other shoppers. I thought, "OMG! No jacket residing on a planet of our gravitation can purposely posses such weight." I managed to inspect it for fit and form finding that I must compliment my dead self for his excellent taste. It fit like a glove.

Time out—here is another expression that makes little sense. I have yet to find a pair (actually two) of gloves that fit like a glove. It must be that foreign artisans with big hands have shorter middle fingers. Every time I purchase hand-wear, my central digit, which is often employed for an important salutatory purpose, is bent in such a way as to match its shorter kin. Do not fear. It takes but a few entries for my extremity to protrude through its confines. It is then all the more conspicuous for its purpose.

A Singular Leather Jacket

The proprietor priced the pristine leather jacket at $10. I was indeed in an uncomfortable situation. As you may have accidentally ascertained, the focus of this story was intended to be my inherent thriftsmanship. I mustn't set a precedent that would besmirch my frugal brethren past and present: the purchase of two commodities at one garage sale without haggling. The hostess may have a video security system. What if she were to broadcast my crime on Highlander YouTube?

As there were at least fifteen patrons who had caught sight of my extraordinary find, I dared not quibble and once again departed from required practices. I did as the jacket had suggested and asked the Dish's assistance in transporting it to the checkout. The dozen shirts, the half dozen pairs of jeans, (I promise not to get into that rant again) and the singular leather jacket that were all once mine are now mine again, although knowing me as I do, probably not at a cheaper price.

Upon homecoming, as I placed the newly purchased jacket within my leather jacket storage facility to wait for the appropriate season, I could not help but speculate about the sheer size of the herd sacrificed to supply the construction materials for such a collection.

It's a new day. The deceased me is interred and the contemporary me is seeking a jacket to stave off the November chills. Upon opening the closet door, in greeting, I said, "Oh, there you are, my $10 weighty leather jacket." As I put it on, it tried to do to my shoulders as it had done to that unfortunate clothes hanger so many months previous. I encouraged myself by stating, "I'm a manly man who is able to bear the weight of this insightfully purchased leather jacket and the consequences of its official Harley Davidson emblem."

Before venturing into the winter's cold, I determined to produce a prideful photograph of our combined fortitude. As Cora and her visiting sister, Bev, had in preplanned malice deserted me for the day, it was my responsibility to bring about the portrait of my jacket and me. I walked us into the bathroom to engage the mirror's assistance in the photographic process.

I found it necessary to switch on all of the bathroom lights. Otherwise the Dish's outdated camera insisted on flashing. The flash produced a picture with an aura over my face much like the famous painting of the guy in a bowler hat with a green apple stuck on his nose. In other pictures, the aura rested on my shoulder, similar to the fairy in *Peter Pan*.

After deleting my first fourteen fruitless attempts I finally created a picture that accentuated our bad-boy persona, a façade that may one day assist in our arrest. I set aside that concern later that evening when the Dish requested that I wear my jacket into the bedroom.

 While the jacket and I were in the bathroom, I once again found reason for pause. In the near future, I must submit to a physical examination. I am, therefore, fasting to lose a gross or two of poundage, an example the jacket should take to heart. For my own piece of mind, I stepped upon the bathroom scale while wearing the jacket and again without same. The leather appliance weighed nearly ten pounds. I dare not wear it to my appointment. The lame-ass nurse always weighs me fully clothed (both she and me).

This morning, I treated Cora and Bev to breakfast before they disappeared into the ether on another shopping foray. I was pleased to wear a Nike t-shirt, a pair of blue jeans and a singular leather jacket, all frugally purchased by me twice.

Before our repast, I had sorted through a stack of old newspapers and found the two dollar per meal discount coupon distributed by Angus's Pub and Grill for Scottish gentlemen of discerning taste with visiting in-laws.

# # # # #

Afterthoughts

I commented to Cora, "I'm sure going to miss garage sale season. I found some great deals this year, but I didn't find an authentic antique like they do on *Antiques Road Show*."

Cora replied, "Bring a mirror."

# # #

Forget About It

While gently aging, I've found that my memory slips more often than my tongue. I could write a book about all that I've forgotten. On the positive side, a good share of the time, I don't remember that I don't remember. I'm not sure how important it is for me to recall that Axle Ross is the lead singer of Guns N' Roses or that John Hancock signed the Constitution in cursive or that Lindsay Slohand starred in the TV movie *Liz N' Dick*. Even so, it's good information to have when I need it.

It's not fair to blame aging for my poor memory. More likely it's due to overindulgence in homemade, chocolate, banana, root beer milkshakes, malted milk balls, and a Scandinavian woman. I read somewhere, I think, that neurologists could perform a brain scan and discover other causes of my memory loss. That'd be a worthwhile procedure if it'd help me find my blender, candy jar, and Cora, my Norwegian spouse.

I'm making efforts to assist whatever memory remains within my software. I purchased a seven-day pill container that holds two innocuous pills in each day's slot, a low-dose aspirin, and an herb something or other. I'm proud to announce that one week's worth of pills now only lasts for three weeks. Every morning, I floss and brush my teeth and shave my face during the same bathroom visit. That way, later in the day, I can stroke my chin and know if I cleaned my teeth or not.

I've developed a work checklist that I write out on Saturday evening for the following week. I draw a line through each reminder once the task is complete and add the forgotten jobs to the following week's list.

Oh, sugar! I just spilled some milkshake onto my computer keyboard. Eh, just forget about it.

I've created Microsoft Excel checklists, such as Forest Visit and Camping Checklist, Exercise Workout Checklist, and Website Password Checklist. I'll add one of those three examples to the end of this story. After each entry on the checklists is a blank space for me to check off the item when it's packed, completed, or entered. I herein resolve to create a checklist of my checklists to help me remember each checklist and to print, post or attach the needed checklist.

Cora, where are my malted milk balls? Cora, Cora…

# # # # #

AFTERTHOUGHTS

My hair turned gray so gradually that I still think it's brown.

# # #

I must remember not to store tubes of toothpaste and hemorrhoid cream in the same drawer. Crest Mint is not soothing.

# # #

I don't have much in common with my pocket comb other than missing teeth.

# # #

My daughter-in-law jokingly set me up with a membership to "Bedwetters Anonymous." I received mailings for years, which eventually stopped about the time I needed them.

# # #

#

I should know by now to open the bathroom door before I put on hand lotion.

#

If I didn't set it down where it shouldn't be, then it must be where it's supposed to be.

#

Our front hallway has a coat closet and a small bathroom. This morning, I entered the closet to the wrong purpose. Fortunately, I didn't find a lid to lift and retreated to the proper facility, wherein I found my jacket, hat, and gloves.

#

I can't remember where I left my car keys last night, but I can remember our home phone number from when I was five years old: Jackson 95953.

#

I must be getting old. While taking a much-deserved nap, I dreamt about eating a tuna fish sandwich. At times, I dream about women too, but, generally, they aren't happy to be there.

#

A few days back, I put a sign over the candy jar that says, "Eat an apple." So today, I ate a grapefruit. Nobody's going to tell me what to do!

#

KING GEORGE I VIGNETTES

KING GEORGE I, AN INTRODUCTION

King George I, although the son of star-crossed lovers, a border collie of impeccable lineage and a common spaniel, demonstrated exceptional intelligence and a noble bearing, granting us the freedom to address him as George, but rebuffing such pet names as Georgie or "Here boy."

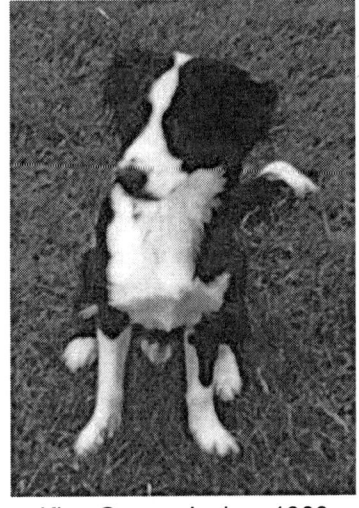

King George I, circa 1988

Upon his initial homecoming, Cora introduced the seven-month-old, newly enthroned monarch to the front yard of his kingdom and our sons, the court jesters, Jerry, age 14, Andy, age 9, and Toby, age 7, who were engaged in a wrestling match. With a hearty guffaw, George leaped into the fray as if he had forever reigned among us. Our cat, Kitty Patrol, so named due to his black-and-white patrol car color scheme, was at first a bit rebellious in the King's presence. After a few nose-to-nose confrontations, the two agreed upon coexistence rather than conflict.

Our family lived within a rural housing development that boasted one-acre parcels. George promptly ascertained his fiefdom's boundaries and disdained a tether. He was, though, much in favor of foreign exploration. The word "walk" elicited a Georgian ballet accompanied by a collar tag concerto. We determined, henceforth, to utter the word in hushed tones, opting to spell it, forwards, backwards and oft times substituting synonyms. All such strategies were as swiftly rendered ineffectual.

The celestial music of jingling car keys educed much the same choreography. No suppression of said percussion instruments sufficed in quelling George's enthusiasm. Welcoming the wind outside of his chauffeured Ford Pinto's rear window with open mouth and lolling tongue was a temptation beyond this monarch's self-control.

KING GEORGE I, THE GLEANER

George elevated gleaning to a kingly art form. During our family meals, no genus or species of victuals escaping the round table found sanctuary on the floor. George's sharply honed hunting instincts, with snout to the floor and rapid nasal gasps, helped him ambush every food fugitive. We dubbed such behavior "snarfing." Subsequent to the capture of all scraps, George was not beyond begging for more. One instance is oft times recalled, much to George's chagrin.

While snacking on dill pickle slices, Cora gave in to George's pleas. The slick slice slid slightly past his dentition before its unceremonious expulsion. George beheld the discharged pickle and Cora in equal disgust as if to say, "How dare you?"

Cora countered, "You asked for it. Now you eat it!" George displayed a most uncharacteristic down-hearted visage, leaned toward the repulsive pickle, snarfed it up, traipsed into the living room and curled up in seclusion.

KING GEORGE I, THE AVENGER

George and I, having comparable culinary inclinations, shared the love of ice cream. When not in public view, we preferred dining directly from the box.

During our first indulgence, we virtually emptied a half-gallon container of Kemp's French Vanilla. For the sole purpose of entertainment at George's expense, I set the open carton with its dregs on the floor. George's ice cream lust defeated his desire for dining decorum. Indubitably aware of the certain outcome, he jammed his face into the box up to his ears, allowing little hope of extrication. Offering scant complaint while dining, George wandered about, haphazardly swinging his encased head, encountering random obstacles.

After exhausting the ice cream remnants and realizing his shame, George pleaded for help. I removed the beleaguered box and, as if not sufficiently demeaned, Kitty Patrol took advantage and administered a thorough tongue lashing upon George's stained ears.

George appreciated a practical joke as much as any other sovereign and soon found the means to avenge his honor. A day or so after his ice cream humiliation, George offered his companionship, and feigned interest in my entertainment selection as he lay upon the floor between the television set and me. He subtly rearranged his position, as if uncomfortable, then lifted his tail and unleashed a senses-shattering, category-5 ice cream fart from such proximity that the effluvium swept my hair back.

The three court jesters fell on the floor contorted in laughter. Cora, reclined upon the couch, laughed herself comatose. George glanced back over his left shoulder, a sly smile on his face, and sauntered into the kitchen.

I, the deserving recipient of George's reprisal, followed as I thought, "This is not over." Peering through watering eyes, I located the grocery list posted on the refrigerator and wrote, "Half-gallon Kemp's New York vanilla ice cream."

KING GEORGE I, THE SPORTSMAN

Over time, King George I and Kitty Patrol grew from mere tolerance to unabashed friendship. Kitty luxuriated in George's spa-like, back rub tongue baths. George reveled in Kitty's schizoid personality—one moment rambunctious, the next compliant. Together, they created an indoor ovoid race track that traversed the hardwood dining room floor, the vinyl-tiled kitchen area, the oak entryway, and the carpeted living room.

A customary steeplechase began as Kitty stationed himself on the end table adjacent the living room couch. As George nonchalantly passed the starting gate, Kitty swatted him on the crown and took off upon the path.

We spectators urged, "Get Kitty, George!" George dashed across the carpet, gaining ground until encountering the dining room floor, where he invariably skidded into the round table, dining chairs, or the wall. All the while, his feet relinquished none of their speed, 20 toenails searching for traction. Once in control, he was off through the kitchen, finding the same result on both the hallway turn and the club house turn into the living room.

George realized Kitty's unfair advantage, mounting the round table, kitchen counters, front hall benches and living room furniture, but rarely complained. Neither the participants nor the fans declared a victor.

George suckered for the "fetch the ball" game, twice, expressing his viewpoints in no uncertain terms.

"Mister, you are easily entertained. What's the point? Where's the challenge? If you throw away that ball and then think better of it, then retrieve it yourself."

Ah, but the "battle for the stick" game was an entirely different matter. The stick—any stick we both coveted—when pitched into the distance, engendered a lopsided competition. Because I exhibited speeds a few kilometers/hour less than George's mocking trot, he was a certain bet to gain the object. I believe George felt bad for his single-minded behavior and, on one occasion, allowed me to win.

As George did not appreciate my ensuing victory dance, he sought to shame me during the following challenge. Having regained the stick, he dropped the captive, inviting me to grab it. I demonstrated no such compulsion. George backed away as if to say, "I'll grant thee a head start, Sir Sidle." He then taunted me further by lying down. That strategy having failed, His Eminence looked away as if not the least bit concerned by my proximity. George's final affront was to simulate sleep. That insult cost him the prize.

When practicable, George preferred water sports above all else. Along a section of our frequented hiking path coursed a slender stream. As we approached, George's typical zigzag cruising pattern gave way to a straight-arrow dash for the rivulet. He sprang into the shallows, creating whirlpools, prancing pretentiously, presenting sticks, and encouraging me to join in his revelry. Disappointed by my apathy, George sat down mid-stream, not willing to disembark until His Majesty so pleased.

George's homeland boasted fine gullies roadside. During a rain storm of any distinction, and after his recital of "The Rite of Spring" ballet, George raced through the thigh-high moats unhinging his lower jaw, slicing the water's surface, ever so more exuberant as I joined in. Subsequent to either of these soggy amusements and prior to palace admission, the King and I spent quality time together air-drying on the portico.

SHARING THE COVERS

As newlyweds, circa 1971, Cora and I had little experience sharing the covers. I've come to believe that Cora's uncommon strength as a northern Minnesota Norwegian farm girl earned her a private berth in the attic of their family's 1890s farm house.

After a night or two of experimentation, Cora claimed the right side of our double bed and left me with the left. As seasoned single sleepers, we both instinctively sought to own all of the covers.

One night, while sleeping on her left side facing away from me, Cora rolled to her right to recover the covers and "accidentally" elbowed me in the left eye socket. The eye and I didn't see it coming. My wraithlike wail and shortsighted swearing undoubtedly opened all eyes in the apartment complex (except for the one full of elbow). Cora leapt out of bed and hit the lights with a left uppercut.

As thrifty newlyweds, we didn't own a steak to use as a countrified cold compress. Instead, we made do with smashed ice cubes wrapped in a dish towel even so my eye swelled shut.

Later that day, as the bruise blossomed strikingly, my co-workers offered up all of the sympathy that one would expect from a crew of blithering rednecks.

During the 42 years since that adornment, Cora has bestowed upon me many a figurative black eye. This story has earned me another. I needn't be concerned about sharing the covers this evening.

#####

AFTERTHOUGHTS

After being scolded, I said, "When we were newly married, as in this story, you didn't mind my scratchy whiskers."

She answered, "When we were newly married, as in this story, you didn't have whiskers."

#

Now That's Just Not Fair

The urgent care doctor said, "Your shivering, fever, and foot pain are the results of an infection, most likely cellulitis. How did you injure your foot?"

I replied, "I don't know for sure. The symptoms began this morning when my wife Cora and I learned that Obamacare cancelled my health insurance policy as of October 15th instead of November 1st as agreed."

He sympathized, "Now that's just not fair."

Within three days and as many oral antibiotics, my left foot grew from a size 13 to a size 17 with a color scheme that mimicked a summer sunset over our forested land.

Dr. Shirley M. Young, my primary care physician, or PCP (an interesting acronym), sent me to the emergency room. Five family medicine (FM) doctors descended upon me and asked a myriad of questions while they covered my torso with stethoscopes. Two of them felt it necessary to take turns performing a prostate exam upon my person while the others observed. (I'm still not clear as to what that had to do with my swollen foot.)

A nurse installed an IV in my right arm and attached an udder of the antibiotic, Vancomycin. She then had me lie upon a mobile bed and stationed it near the emergency room exit door. There I patiently awaited a room for 183 minutes—not that I was counting.

With little experience beyond birth, I was ill at ease about a hospital stay, a probing pentad of family physicians, an IV and its pouch of drugs, and my gaudy mega-foot. As a result, sleep eluded me until 1:30 a.m.

At 2 a.m. a nurse woke me to ask my birth date and replaced the antibiotics sac. She returned at 5 a.m. to weigh me on a freestanding scale. My body didn't feel like waking nor did my foot feel like standing. I trust that she was satisfied with an error factor of plus or minus 10 percentage points, as are most political pollsters.

At 6 a.m. I had a 45-minute consultation with an MRI machine. It looked like a metallic tractor tire and sounded as if a herd of hamsters were running inside the wheel dragging its lug nuts.

The MRI tech was aware of the machine's idiosyncrasies and supplied me with a set of radio headphones. She asked what genre of music I enjoy. I requested classic rock. She then placed a squeeze ball in my left hand so that I could alert her if I had any needs during the procedure. I endured five minutes of Christian rock before I crushed it.

Two hours of antibiotic infusions every twelve hours created a dilemma. The bathroom was over there and I was over here. As experienced as the nurses were, I was uncomfortable about requesting transport to the bathroom and stabilization while I targeted the throne. Instead, I made use of my untrustworthy garage sale crutches and found that they still reveled in snagging upon random items, which in everyday life would pose no threat. After bestowing upon them several popular and a few lesser known obscenities, I hopped on one foot like a drugged koala into the bathroom and back to the bed before the hospital staff was any the wiser.

That night, the crutches and I came to an understanding. They would function for my functions and I would keep them from deep space flight.

After just two days in the hospital, I developed a routine: a crutch-assisted bathroom trip every two hours 24/7, 6 a.m. blood draw, breakfast, read, doctor visits, lunch, infusion, vitals checked, doctor visits, read, anti-blood clot injection, dinner, read, midnight infusion and vitals checked.

To my surprise, I discovered some advantages to hospital life. I was encouraged to wear pajamas all day and go commando. Someone made my food to order and had it delivered to my bedside. The TV remote was hardwired to the nightstand. The personnel are apologetic when they caused me pain, unlike someone I know who lives at our home (whose name I won't mention in this sentence, otherwise I'll be hurting).

I also discovered several possible private pleasure positions thanks to this creative electric bed and its gel mattress. I'm not sure what good they will do me though. Even if we did own an electric bed and a gel mattress, I'm sure I wouldn't be in charge of the controls.

After three days, my foot looked like a voluminous violet vegetable. Therefore, the FM doctors asked the infectious disease (ID) doctors for their opinions. Early in the afternoon, the head of the ID department arrived with four residents in tow. I showed them a picture of my foot from three days previous. One of the residents raised his hands and shouted, "Jesus." I believe his outburst expressed shock rather than an attempt at spiritual healing.

Fortunately, the ID posse passed on multiple prostate exams and discussed their thoughts in private outside my open door. Not long thereafter, a handsome orthopedic (bone specialist) resident arrived to check my foot. The nurses flushed as he passed and fanned themselves by whatever means available. He felt my foot at length and decided that my bones didn't need his further attention. Just as I'd finished fanning myself with a pillow case, his boss stopped by to confirm the finding.

Within the hour, a ravishing rheumatology resident (female) stopped in to check my ankle joint. I was a bit saddened to learn that I didn't have arthritis. Nonetheless, her boss ordered a pelvic x-ray. I couldn't help but think, "Five FM doctors, five ID doctors, two rheumatology doctors, two orthopedic doctors, and enough nurses to set up a rugby league. Each with his or her own set of tests to perform. Each concerned and driven to come up with an answer. And on top of that a pelvic x-ray! OB-GYN can't be far behind."

I hadn't had that much attention since my wedding in 1971. But that was of a different kind. Cora's wedding guests cut loose with a rash of comments, "He doesn't look Norwegian. Betcha he's from the city, college boy no doubt. Betcha he doesn't hunt deer or spear nordern pike. Ya, or can green beans, fry his steaks or boil coffee. Uffda, will ya look at the size of those feet!"

As I lay on the hospital bed for hours on end, I developed a rash on my back. In order to block out the in-law memories that the chafing revived, I dove into a humorous book, *A Hitchhikers Guide to the Galaxy*. I laughed out loud several times. Within minutes, Dr. Bhopal, a psychiatry resident, stopped by. In my defense, I read this quote, "The ships hung in the sky in much the same way that bricks don't."

Twenty minutes later, a nurse arrived with an additional pouch of drugs.

The FM doctors decided to cease the infusions and start me on an oral antibiotic called Doxycylin and send me home the next day. I remember dating a girl with a similar sounding name in college. If it's as effective as she, then I'll be out of here tonight. No matter, the ID doctors overruled the FM doctors and said I'd be staying another five days for continued infusions.

I was feeling down when a delightful nurse's assistant stopped in and asked if I would like her to help me take a shower. Although tempted, I replied, "No, thank you. My wife would be sorely disappointed if she missed out."

When Cora arrived, I made mention of the conversation. She replied, "Sure I'll help. Where are the scrub brush and the Brillo pads?"

While Cora buffed my hives, I proposed, "We're on the top floor of the hospital. What say we join the hospital's version of the Mile-high Club?" Alas, it's now day twelve and I'm on my fifth new antibiotic. This infection has a long way to go before it becomes as difficult to conquer as Cora.

With the passage of time and ninety-six bi-hourly bathroom visits, the FM and ID doctors had specialists install a long-term IV called a PICC line, supplied a leg cushion with instructions to keep my foot elevated above heart level while seated, and sent me home with a prescription to return daily *ad infinitum* for antibiotic infusions.

A physical therapist stopped by before my departure to offer some tips on relearning to walk. To help in the process, she gifted me with a brand-new walker minus the yellow tennis balls. With gifts, instructions, and prescriptions in hand, I said to Cora, "Upon my homecoming, there are a couple of other gifts that I'd appreciate."

She gibed, "You must be on drugs."

Since I've been home, I've learned that being temporarily disabled gives me so much not to do. With that in mind, I'm trying to walk. I expect to have a reasonable gait within the week. Ballet will have to wait until my dance slippers fit and I regain enough weight to fill out my tights.

While seated without the tutu and my foot in the stratosphere, I commented optimistically, "Life has its challenges. We'll handle them all."

Cora walked over, patted me on the head and said, "Your hair is thinning."

I mumbled, "Now that's just not fair."

# # # # #

AFTERTHOUGHTS

Today I had quite a list of things not to do. I chose three of them. The rest can wait until tomorrow.

#

Hoping to gain a few pounds, I must compliment myself and say that I did a terrible job of not eating today.

#

While Cora sorted the Christmas decorations, I asked if I could play with her ornaments.

She replied, "You've already had one hospital stay in the past month."

#

ROMANCE IN BLOOM

As a third-year psychology student studying at the University of Minnesota in 1970, I was surprised to find that my education and my vast 20-year life experience did not prepare me for the cross-cultural experience of courting Cora Sue Johnson, a blue-eyed-blond, Norwegian, northern Minnesota farm girl.

Ms. Johnson and I met June 27th, four weeks and two days after her 18th birthday and simultaneous departure from her small hometown. We visited her family often during our first summer together. Ma, Pa, and the boys lived in a rented 1890s farm house for which they paid $25 per month, a severe drain on their finances.

Pa worked as a handy man with Cora Sue's elder brother, Richie. Ma was a housewife employed part-time frying burgers and pouring 50-cent beers at the local bar and grill, Boo and Ruby's. Cora's little brother Glen stood 5 foot 8 and packed 130 lbs. of lean beef, which belied his ten years of age. Bevy,

Cora and Rick at her parents' farmhouse (1971)

the eldest sibling, preceded Cora Sue in the exodus from their hometown.

During our August visit, Cora Sue and I planned a nature walk at a special place. (The cramped quarters of her family's farm house were not conducive to romance.)

Cora Sue drove her rusted 1965 Ford Custom along several unpaved roads until I was fairly well lost and a bit panicked. I held the city-boy opinion that dirt roads should not be traversed at freeway speeds. She was well pleased with her exhibition that filled our wake with a cloud of debris and marked our trail all the way to the railroad tracks just this side of Inspiration Peak.

The railroad bed above the boggy ditches split the dense woods, which seemed to reunite in the distance. An inspiring clear blue sky mirrored Cora Sue's eyes. The refreshing breeze persuaded the swamp grass to polka but could not convince the tamarack to join in. We held hands and spoke only through our touch as we walked the tracks.

Unexpectedly, Cora Sue let go of my hand and scurried down the embankment to a grouping of wild flowers. I wondered as she thinned the display and crafted an attractive arrangement of honeysuckle. Could she be so romantic? Is the bouquet for me or Ma or perhaps just for her own enjoyment?

Upon regaining the railroad path, Cora Sue inverted the bouquet and gave it a strong shake as she might with an overburdened dust mop.

I inquired, "What's that about?"

Cora Sue's eyes smiled as she answered, "Oh, I'm just shaking out the bugs."

She then righted the bouquet and reached within as if it was a bag of movie theater popcorn. She plucked several blooms, popped them into her mouth and, true to her upbringing, was cautious not to speak while dining.

As we continued our stroll along the tracks on that peaceful afternoon, I wondered whether Cora Sue was entranced by the vista or in search of dessert.

A BEDTIME PRIMER:
MAY YOU REST IN PEACE

The evening should be a relaxing escape from work, a chance to visit with the family, enjoy a meal, read or watch TV, followed by a good night's sleep while interruptive cell phones and iPods swirl in the commode. But who among us merely falls upon the bed and conks out? The elaborate bedtime tribulations we all endure are ingrained, often obsessive and difficult to amend.

Cora "the Dish" and I married in 1971, just after my graduation from college. While dating, I didn't need to understand the subtle intricacies of mixed gender sleeping. Dormitories were segregated for either male or female occupation. It required stealth to enter feminine apartments. Each housed a minimum of two lovelies, an outcome that was well worth the risk. Yes, Dish, I'm already dreaming.

BEDTIME A.D.D.
It has been a long day, but I yearn to watch Alanis Morissette on *The Tonight Show*. That's an hour and 28 minutes from now. I might succeed if I initiate my bedtime preparations immediately. Where's my cordless shaver? Ok, here it is. I must rid my face of scratchy stubble, otherwise no bedtime kisses or snuggles. What, it's out of juice? I'll hit the shower (same reason) while the shaver recharges. Then I'll proceed with dental care: floss, brush, and mouthwash (same reason). Next, apply moisturizing lotion to smooth out my abrasive hands... Set the alarm clock. Verify that the Kleenex box is full. Position a notebook and pen on the bedside stand for middle of

A Bedtime Primer: May You Rest in Peace

the night business ideas. Activate the white noise appliance. Turn down the bed. Get dressed again.

If I strut directly into the living room after my shower, Cora will laugh and our nosy neighboring spinster will want some sugar. Walk around the house. Confirm that the outside lights are turned off, the doors are locked, and the windows coverings are closed.

Check the computer for urgent emails, stock reports, and communications from NASA. Crack the last can of Coors Light "the Dish" hid behind the pot of leftover chili.

I missed Alanis and "the Dish" is sound asleep.

BEDTIME CONCERNS:
- Fashionable sleep wear, makeup removal and overnight hairstyle protection are not my concerns.
- The bed right of center belongs to Cora. It can be shared under the correct set of circumstances. I have yet to discover what they may be.
- A pillow stationed between my knees assists my slumber, otherwise those bickering, bony buggers keep each other awake.
- Due to my side-sleep position and my right of center problem, I wrap my arms around a full-size pillow to keep my shoulders from caving in.

BEDTIME WISDOM:
- Caution, there are times that women do not wish to be ogled on their journey toward bed.
- Don't replace her bedside stand glass of water with vodka.
- Don't fart beneath the covers.

BEDTIME ANNOYANCES:

- Most can be overcome by the use of one or more of these four initiatives: adaptation, harsh words, drugs, and firearms.

- As a younger man I slept like death on the forest floor. Now a wrinkle in the mattress pad is troublesome. "The Dish" advises, "For pity's sake, take a pill or something."

- So what if she snores. Purchase a set of ear plugs. They're available at most firearms dealers. I have attempted on numerous occasions to gently wake my wife during her susurrations (I'll wait while you look up that word), demonstrating a below-average learning curve and a questionable gene pool according to "the Dish."

  This imprudent practice has accounted for the lion's share of the bruises I have earned during our years of marital merriment. For unattached males, I respectfully suggest that you check your babe's credentials before cohabitation. Avoid females with Judo, Tai Chi or World Wrestling Federation experience. Tae Kwon Do—dump her after your first date, preferably by text or email.

- I have not yet discovered why our backyard neighbor insists on watering his Shetland pony dog at freaking 4 a.m. and then recalling him with a two-handed, four-fingered, wolf whistle that would startle the throng at the Super Bowl stadium during a 4th-quarter interception.

- His back porch, multi-megawatt search light remains illuminated and shines on our window all night long, thanks to a motion sensor that's activated by fleeting, subatomic particles. The solution to this problem is adaptation. On second thought, screw adaptation, my neighbor, his searchlight and his dog. Where's my pellet gun?

- There's just not enough ball room in my tidy whities. Rather a vulgar problem, but handled here with aplomb. Plan in advance and wear boxers.

- Last night I wore boxers and woke with one wicked wedgie.

A Bedtime Primer: May You Rest in Peace

- Wring out your shower washcloth before you retire. I guarantee you'll employ harsh language after the 44th drip that occurs precisely thirteen seconds after the 43rd drip.

- I'm the one who wanted to eek out one more season from our forced-air furnace. It generates more innovative noises than a prairie profuse with insects and Campfire Girls.

- Speaking of insects, swat that infuriating fly or mosquito before you go to bed. Otherwise your wife will avail herself of all four previously stated initiatives.

- For your own piece of mind, employ bed coverings that are a minimum of one size larger than your mattress. Yes, you will take criticism every morning for the overhang but so much less than the continual, "you hogged all the covers again last night" crap.

- As a child, our family's home was crowded with occupants, a circumstance that required Uncle Bobby and me to share a bed. I don't exaggerate when I state that his toenails had grown unabated since his conception. During Bobby's nightmares, his legs cycled in such a fashion as to qualify him for a position on Lance Armstrong's Tour de France team. His toenails tore into me nightly as if I had bunked with a cornered tomcat. Eventually, I got some guts and punched him in the nose. Choose your own bed partner. Request trimmed toenails before resorting to violence.

- When your side-sleeping wife has an itch on the bottom of her foot, kindly suggest that she use caution when bending her knee.

- Trim the branches of every tree and shrub within a parsec, 3.258 light years, of your residence. Otherwise at 3 a.m., you will hear, "Hubby, wake up! Wake up, Hubby! Do you hear that? Something is scratching at the window."

- If your spouse can't sleep, then neither will you. Be sympathetic if you expect a bed-time companion in the future. Tell her a bedtime story, sing her a lullaby, or give her a backrub.

- Everyone has the perfect position for a great night's sleep. If you plan to employ it, then buy twin beds or stay single.

- Place your eye glasses, car keys, TV remote, cell phone, wallet, and anything else you regularly misplace on your bedside stand. Your wife will laud your wisdom.

- Prevent disruptive nocturnal visits to the bathroom. If you are thirsty within 3 hours of bedtime, forget about it. Have a beer at the office.

- Having not obeyed my advice, curse softly when you stub your toe in the dark while sleep-walking towards the bathroom. Otherwise your wife will laugh herself sick and mock you again, "That's the fifth time this month. I bet, not only did you hit the dresser again, but the same toe. Why don't you move the dresser or put padding on that spot or turn on the light or wear slippers or amputate that toe or stop drinking before bed or buy a bigger bladder or find some coordination." Not that I have ever experienced such an event.

   Oh, here she goes again, "And for goodness (word substitution) sake, turn on the bathroom light, open you eyes and pay attention. Check the toilet seat first. Consider sitting down. No one will know. You might improve your accuracy. Of course a 60/40 success rate whether sitting or standing might be just dreaming on my part."

That's it. I'm tired of writing. I'm going to bed.

# # # # #

AFTERTHOUGHTS

My sister sent me two page-a-day calendars: *Roget's Word a Day for Intellectuals*, and *B.C.'s Joke a Day*.

Cora said, "Place the intellectual calendar by the computer where you write your high-brow stories and the B.C. calendar on your nightstand."

# # #

I've got an Olivia Newton John song playing over and over again in my head. It, it WON'T go away. I'll never get to sleep. I think I'll lick a light socket.

# # #

I just arrived home. If I hurry, maybe I can miss *Wheel of Fortune*.

# # #

I try not to watch the TV before bed. The disturbing commercials for colon health, E.D., and bladder leakage, among others, are enough to make me lose control and require some of the advertised medications. Then again, all those guys in the Cialis commercials are ruggedly handsome, own classic muscle cars, and vacation in cool places. Maybe it'd be worth having their problem.

# # #

Subterranean

As a teenager, my parents relegated me to living quarters beneath our modest home. The only passage to the basement hideaway was a steep staircase punctured into the floor at the convergence of our living room and kitchen. I agreed, in principle, to subsist within the subterranean environment. It seemed the only acceptable alternative to a life scrutinized by a flock of familial females.

Grandma had come to live with us and minister to my two younger sisters while my mother escaped to her part-time job at Abdallah's Candy Company. Dad, our household's only other rational being, spent his life working ungodly hours as far away from home as prudent.

I, an archetypical Morlock as envisioned by H.G. Wells, endured the basement's cold, cracked concrete floor, cinder block walls, overhead floor joists, and the widely dispersed, dreary, dangling light bulbs. Meanwhile, the unappreciative, simple-minded Eloi females occupied the comfy, private bedrooms on the main floor. At least my subterranean companions—the furnace, washer, and dryer—seemed to appreciate the privacy I facilitated by suspending my childhood Davy Crocket bedspread between our alcoves from a bordering beam.

Over time, I grew accustomed to and took advantage of the appliances' idiosyncrasies. The furnace, with its gyrating, off-balance fan, sent irregular heat blasts through the single basement vent that I'd incised into its creaking ductwork with a tin snips. The women soon caught wind of my breakthrough and discovered the system made for an incomparable hairdryer.

The doddering Mr. Washer never failed to disappoint my quest for rest. Mrs. Dryer-Washer, often times accompanied her mate's staccato with a discordant, loose-change lullaby. With each counterpoint, I added the percussion instruments, said coins, to my Dairy Queen Milkshake fund.

During the summer season, I enjoyed the cooler temperatures of life underground and gained a healthy respect for my soul mates: centipedes, spiders, mice and the occasional kangaroo rat. As innovative subterranean home builders, they bested the comforts provided by the Troglodytes that fabricated my hermitage.

With every rainfall, the groundwater seeped through cinder-block fissures, window-well edgings, windows only in the strictest definition, substratum cracks and up through the floor drain. Drain, yeah, that word works. Along with the groundwater, castoffs from our overflowing septic system skulked their way into my live-in wading pool.

Dad used to joke, "Rick, just stick a sail in 'em and float 'em on by."

During my first rainfall as a Morlock, I found comfort while snuggled up in my roll-away bed until I arose the next morning yet awash in the dreams of another successful babe hunt. I swung my bare feet over the bed edge and unwittingly sank them into several inches of sewage. Then the panic struck.

I slogged hurriedly over to my foot locker with the false bottom and rescued my secret stash of 1960s *Playboy* magazines. I prayed that Ursula Andres, Marilyn Monroe, Jayne Mansfield, and the babes were yet in their full glory. Finding nothing more than the damage sustained in previous viewings, I henceforth sheathed them in prophylactic plastic wrap.

All subterranean heroes, such as Batman, have at least one arch-enemy. In my case, the Joker, the Riddler, the Penguin, *et al* morphed into skanky, good-for-nothing, hairy-legged, pointy-assed crickets. Without invitation, one nemesis per night invaded my sanctuary between the hours of bedtime and breakfast, and incessantly chirped its expectant mating song to me alone.

Searching them out in the shadows was a challenge not to be assumed by the easily discouraged or the faint of heart. The spineless buggers hid themselves in the dark, dank recesses that could be found anywhere in our basement but, most notably, behind the spider-webbed spaces where our home's wooden walls rested on the basement's cinder blocks.

As my teenage height was about thirty percent on the underside of average, I stood barefoot on a metal folding chair, held tight to the cinder-block ledges, and clamped a flashlight between my teeth, which by the way, made my curses difficult for the vermin to decipher. If I got lucky and found the miscreant, I'd squish its brittle, boneless body with a glob of my sisters' wet laundry.

Since hunting crickets only added to my sleeplessness, I sought out other approaches to insecticide. I hit upon an idea and bought several Dutch Cleanser-type cans of insect powder replete with the popular, pulverized pesticides of the day. I dusted every elevated horizontal surface within my grotto, save my bed, with enough toxic talcum to kill off a legion of zombies, let alone a marauding cricket.

A hazardous haze of poisonous pollutants formed and eerily drifted above the swampy swill. It metamorphosed the ambiance of my digs into that of a marshy mausoleum. The fog irritated my eyes, lightened my hair, disinfected my skin, and cauterized my lungs. I felt invincible, ruthless as I stood ankle deep in the sludge. I rubbed my hands together in ghoulish delight when a cricket's amorous chant transformed into a dirge. I knew that the interloper would never get lucky and would soon become one with the ooze.

In retrospect, I must pay homage to my subterranean upbringing with its sewage, noxious fog, and cohabitants. It transformed me into the man that I am today—sensitive (to sunlight), exhibiting pale skin, sallow toenails, burly body parts, and an unusual resistance to the effects of toxins, pathogens, deodorants, unrequited serenades, and familial females.

#####

Sup and Spew

Cora and I dined last night at a well-known Sup and Spew restaurant franchise. Cora enjoyed her repast but enough of her thoughts. Later that evening, I composed this critique while my feast's foul flavor festered.

I shall commence with a well-deserved dissection of the side salad, which was surely tossed within the reclining chef's navel grotto. Pasty pink rings of Italian onion crowned the salad. I unabashedly picked and flicked them beneath an unoccupied neighboring table.

With the onions gone, I viewed sallow shreds of toe cheese and gold crown-cracking croutons assuredly resurrected from Pompeii, all of which lay upon the salad's surface like so much volcanic debris. Terminally flaccid lettuces lay shamefully beneath the crust forming a crater in the salad saucer. A sextet of voluptuous vegetables could not have restored their turgidity.

Mingled within the dysfunctional lettuces were tomato husks diced to mask their prepubescent pallor and four lengths of dizzying, rotund rotini that exhibited more counterclockwise coils than a water park slide. Odiferous blue cheese duck-butter dressing slimed the muddle. Here was little more than the regurgitations of a toothless yak. (It must have eaten some of the croutons.)

Oh, lest I forget, the condiment cup was brimming with cottage cheese lipo-sucked from the chef's namesake thighs.

My appetite was taken aback. Even so, it hoped for satiety from the patty melt sandwich. In the interest of self-preservation, before ingesting, I peeled back the rye-scented, soggy toast. Underneath, a greasy dish-sponge burger rested amid jaundiced, cheesy sweater shields dripping with Thousand

Island dressing. Something resembling sautéed onions squirmed in the midst.

Who can screw up catsup? It's in a regulated F.D.A. inspected bottle, for crying out loud! Yet, when I squeezed the inverted container, it ripped loose an incessant fart that attracted the reproachful leers of every diner, waitress, and busboy in the eatery. Even the salad chef managed to glance away from his navel contemplations. My gestures of innocence were ineffectual. The hapless, baptized burger foundered in a translucent sea of tomato ketchup plasma.

Even my carbonated beverage sucked! Upon its surface drifted citrus-scented, sulfur-shaded spume, along with a few ensnared ice shards.

I shoved my meal aside, nearly half of it uneaten. Succeeding succinct remarks I expressed to our waitress, she removed the repugnant remnants from the table and their cost from our check, but not the tang from my palate. A savor survived that I imagined would be somewhat analogous to the aftertaste of dining on Scotty Pippin's NBA championship sweat socks. (I was going to write jock strap, but that would've been vulgar.)

In apology for my dreadful dinner, the waitress offered a free piece of pie to go from their decadent selection: sour cream rabbit raisin, steaming cow patty chocolate pecan, caramel horse apple revelation and dingle-berry cheesecake, packed into a wedgie-shaped Styrofoam container. At first I declined. Then, an idea blossomed. I recanted and asked the waitress to choose a piece for me. Upon homecoming, I fed the offal to our neighbor's trio of yoke-yanking yappy Yorkies—Yoda, Yogi and Fred.

# # # # #

WARSH

Dear family and friends,

Cora and I have just returned home from visiting the Johnsons in their northern Minnesota hometown of Henning, where comfort is found in continuity. Ma Johnson, Cora's mom, as yet lives with her son Richie on his 160-acre farm. Ma is still as Norwegian as ever, in excellent health at age 82, and as feisty as I have learned to expect having been married to her daughter for 33+ years.

After warm greetings, I stretched out upon the living room carpet and took pleasure in listening to classical Henningese conversation. Ma's accent persists, adding an "r" to words that begin with "wa" such as Warshington or Wardena, whether they deserve it or not.

Ma Johnson and Cora at Richie's home (2004)

Ma updated Cora on all the latest local events—who had died, who didn't, who wants to, who had visited whom, who moved from this corner to that, and how many deer and turkeys had been seen grazing in their front yard pasture. As per normal, Richie disagreed with Ma on most counts and was not shy at presenting his own point of view.

A fair amount of back-and-forthing followed each correction, with an exasperated Ma at times countering Richie's claims with her ultimate Norwegian comeback, "Ohferdumb."

We all went out to dinner that evening at Oakwood Supper Club, located next to Henning's 9-hole, par-36 golf course. Their menu offered your choice of fried shrimp, fried chicken strips, or a fried cheeseburger in a basket with fries and a soda.

A wedding party was happening in the banquet hall on the other side of the dining room's imaginary wall. Lars and Sven Jorgensen, party attendees, were busy putting the moves on two fine-looking kegs of beer. The local entertainer, a Dave Crosby impersonator, was on a break, so we waited half an hour after supper's completion for him to stop primping and sing a few bars. After a minute of his bogus song styling, we bailed out.

Sunday morning, Richie attended a coin collector's auction and spent close to $500 on 55 cents. To his credit, he researched each coin of interest, referencing the latest price guides before he participated in the auction.

While Richie was busy spending money on money, I went for a hike through his 100-acre forest. I found a cast-off deer antler, brought it to Ma, and authored a story as to how I had obtained it.

A buck bounded out of Richie's woodland and attempted to head-butt me. I spun about, dodged to the left and put a head lock on him as he passed. He bawled such a harangue of religious words that I thought he might have been the keynote speaker at last week's Henning Red Hat Lady's revival meeting. I wouldn't let him loose even after he offered further disparaging remarks about my parentage. I was about to bulldog him to the ground when his left antler broke off in my hand and threw me off balance. One of his forward kicks then caught me in the vital statistics. As my grip loosed on his remaining antler, he shook free and fled, flipping me off with his white tail repeatedly as raced around the trees.

Ma was doubtful as to the truth of my account. The story is spot on, every word of it. I have the antler to prove it.

Ma baked turkey and her famous wild apple pie for Sunday dinner. She had gleaned the apples last fall from beneath an immigrant forest dweller. I don't believe the bird was locally harvested (shot or road kill, which is the norm). Coincidentally, there were two wild turkeys perched on the front deck railing. Ma said that her freezer was full. So she let them be.

After dinner, Ma tried to talk Richie out of going ice fishing as the ice was drifting away from shore and honey-combed. Richie assured Ma that he would just walk a plank from shore to the ice and leave the truck behind. His comment earned him a couple of Norwegian expressions, which I understood even without any knowledge of the language. (I had heard something similar from the deer.)

We, without Richie—he was ice fishing—spent the evening visiting while watching the one available TV channel provided by the 30ft. reception tower Richie salvaged from the dump ground. Otherwise the only accessible entertainment was the local Deer Creek (pronounced Deer Crik in Henningese) polka radio station.

Cora and I drove into town Monday morning for breakfast at Lucy's restaurant and pull-tab salon. We discovered that Lucy had sold the business to her daughter and it is now known as Mama Boe's. At the front counter, patrons are expected to sort through the stack of auction handbills before their meal. These auctions are generally held at the estates of retiring farmers who are attempting to fund their golden years by selling vintage tractors, farm furniture, rifles, cattle stanchions, 20-gallon milk cans and other items, which are probably quite saleable in Henning but don't compliment our current décor.

I ordered the Big Otter breakfast, which contained no otter parts, but did offer 3 scrambled eggs, 4 bacon strips, 4 toast halves, 4 sanitary packs of jelly, 2 dinner plate size pancakes, 2 packages of maple syrup, and a mound of freshly fried hash browns all for $3.75. I enjoyed the feed, the full feeling that lasted for days, and the patrons.

Two tables were pushed together to host a group of locals, who took turns shaking a can containing dice then dumping them on the table. The person with the lowest score weathered a fair amount of taunting and bought the next round of coffees. Junior Bloemke, a lifelong Henningite, was involved in the game. He's deaf and can't speak, but managed to make his gibes understood.

After breakfast, Cora and I drove a few miles to visit her Aunt Ruth, who now lives with her son, Ken, and his two children in the small town of Vining. The town is known for its local sculptor's many huge, unique iron artworks. His most famous statute, a giant foot with the big toe tilted upwards, is on display outside the gas station.

When Cora and I began dating, she lived and worked at the Glen Lake State Sanatorium. I did not feel the nurse's dorm was a safe place. At my request, Cora moved in with Aunt Ruth, who at that time lived just a few miles away. I got to know Ruth well during Cora's stay. Ruth has been through some difficult times this past year with the installation of a pacemaker and gall bladder surgery. Thankfully, she's now doing quite well.

We left for home just after noon Monday. We stopped along the way for a late lunch and a piece of pie at the Norse Nook. It was a pleasant drive all the way home as the weather cooperated. We are now unpacked and Cora has called Ma to assure her of our safe arrival. Cora has one day of vacation remaining. She plans to go shopping tomorrow, somewhere far removed from my company. As for me, I plan to go for a bike ride and do the warsh.

Most sincerely,
Rick A. Wehler

# # # # #

THE VIEW

I'm not sure why I've been compelled every Monday morning since my 64th birthday to step on my insensitive bathroom scale. Last week it berated, "I've already warned you twice about devouring six slices of Cora's homemade banana bread before bed, but noooo, you won't listen. For once, try taking my advice to heart instead of your stomach. Throw away the remnants of her banana bread, the big bucket of rocky road ice cream and the kiloton of discounted Halloween candy you have hidden in the basement cabinets. Otherwise, don't expect any sympathy from me in the future."

I mumbled, "Next week I'm skipping Monday."

The scale gibed, "You're too heavy to skip."

Today I'm taking control of my actions in order to win out over the expected Monday morning mocking.

After prying myself away from my warm, snuggling wife, I sit upon the edge of our bed, remove my pajamas, and take several deep breaths to strengthen my resolve. Then into the bathroom I head to eliminate dinner's carafe of Zinfandel and dry-comb my hair to avoid water weight. My eye glasses remain wherever they ended up last night.

You might wonder, "How does he read the scale without his glasses?" By way of my finely calibrated, interactive bathroom scale, a birthday gift from Cora, who programmed its password-protected announcements with Keith Urban's voice.

I dust off the scale and climb aboard. Keith chuckles and, in his Aussie accent, says, "188 pounds! Nice job, lard ass." Taking control of the situation, I shoot back, "Yeah, well, you can smell my feet, and I hope you're enjoying the view from down under."

# # # # #

CHOLESTEROL COUNT

It's difficult for me to comprehend the claim that cholesterol is a calamitous compound when I consider the copious collection of cuisines that contain such a cache of it.

On a warm summer's day, nothing quenches my thirst like a homemade, chocolate, banana, root beer milkshake. I just can't believe that something so tasty could be bad for me.

If you're intrigued by my concoction, then checkout this list of the needed equipment and conditions for its preparation, my time-honored recipe and step-by-step directions for sealing your fate.

EQUIPMENT AND CONDITIONS:

1. A 64oz.-capacity blender. Once you've got the hang of it, refills are easy.
2. An ice cream scoop, because wives discourage the use of their bendable tablespoons.
3. Privacy.
4. A tablespoon.
5. A washcloth and a container of counter cleaner.
6. A DVD player.
7. A burly bib, not one of those wussy types with a picture of a lobster on it.
8. A comfy chair within easy reach of the dishwasher.

CHOLESTEROL COUNT

TIME-HONORED RECIPE:

1. A 5qt. pail (nowadays a 4.13qt. pail) of full-bodied ice cream, not the lite aberration. If you seek to limit calories, sugars, and fats, then you're not on my planet. I prefer New York Vanilla ice cream because it doesn't contain walnuts.
2. A half-gallon jug of chocolate milk, and I don't mean the low-fat drivel (see #1).
3. A 21.8oz. container of Nestle Nesquik chocolate powder, the type that doesn't boast 25% less sugar (see #1). By the way, substituting chocolate protein powder is just wrong.
4. One box of Better Crocker Fudge Brownie Mix, not the low-fat fake (see #1).
5. One ripe banana, peeled.
6. Your daily litany of vitamin pills and prescription drugs, including statins. You won't need the hallucinogen.
7. One 12oz. can of chilled A&W root beer, not the diet drool (see #1).
8. One 13oz. container of Reddiwip Extra Creamy Real Whipped Cream, not the low-fat froth (ditto).
9. One heaping tablespoon of sprinkles, or jimmies if you prefer.
10. One jar of maraschino cherries.

STEP-BY-STEP DIRECTIONS:

1. Set the blender on the counter, not far from an overhanging cabinet and remove the jar lid.
2. Remove your shirt, but keep it close by.
3. Slice the peeled banana into the blender jar.
4. Put the lid on the blender jar, slide it beneath the cabinet, set the dial to puree, and activate.

5. Turn the blender off and remove the lid, in that order, add your pills and repeat #4.

6. Turn the blender off and remove the lid, in that order. If you got confused in the order while awaiting your medications, then make use of #5 in the equipment and conditions list and compliment your foresight in that the cupboard confined the eruption.

7. Prepare the brownie mix and bake per the instructions.

8. Fill the blender to the 48oz. level with scoops of ice cream. Feel free to exercise your right as chef to double dip.

9. Season to taste with at least two tablespoons of Nesquik chocolate powder.

10. Pour in chocolate milk nearly to the top of the heart attack. Fill the remaining space up to ice cream level with root beer, discounting the foam.

11. Place the lid on the blender jar and once again slide it beneath the cabinet.

12. Activate the blender at low speed and increase as your impatience warrants.

13. When the ingredients reach an even yet disquieting consistency, turn off the blender, slide it from beneath the cupboard, and remove the lid.

14. There should be about an inch of space remaining between the milkshake and the top of the blender jar. Fill that with a 4-inch to 6-inch pile of whipped cream and decorate with the sprinkles or jimmies and several maraschino cherries.

15. Disconnect the blender jar from the motor. Put away the motor, the remaining ingredients, and the counter cleaner, etc.

16. Place the dirty dishes in the dishwasher.

17. Turn on the DVD player and activate any one of the *Death Wish* movies.

18. Don your burly bib to keep most of the dribbles from lodging in your chest hair.
19. Sit back in your comfy chair with milkshake in hand and indulge. Make use of a tablespoon instead of a straw due to the sludge-like consistency and periodic pill pieces.
20. You should be finished with your snack well before the oven timer warns that the brownies are done. Reach over and place the blender jar and tablespoons in the dishwasher.
21. Remove your burly bib, wipe off your face, and any additional telltale slop and discard it.
22. Put your shirt back on, tuck it in and remove the brownies from the oven.
23. When the wife arrives, due to the aroma, she'll love that you made brownies for her and will offer you a warm one, thus thawing your brain freeze.

Now that the holiday season is upon me, I've backed off on milkshake consumption to allow room in my cholesterol count for unadulterated eggnog. Did you know that it's currently available in half-gallon jugs? The powers that be should also create a drink box for my convenience while I'm on the road to the deli. I can't wait to dine upon a corned beef, bacon, and Swiss cheese sandwich on toasted, buttered rye bread.

# # # # #

AFTERTHOUGHTS

I tried a low-cholesterol, chocolate soy milkshake tonight. A magazine article said that I shouldn't drink soy milk because it produces estrogen in men and can make them moody. Well, I don't believe that! Do you think these jeans make my butt look fat?

# # #

No More Tears

While driving home after a day clearing invasive autumn olive trees from our woodland property, I began shedding tears. I didn't think they were due to my recently shattered shoulder, the tripping victim of a displaced, disgruntled tree-climbing vine, or even undue emotion, but rather a stench that I likened to farm-fresh doggy doo emanating from within Miss Penny Purebred, my tan 1997 Ford Taurus.

I sniffed my armpits. Finding them uncharacteristically innocent and fairly certain that my tidy whities remained so, I commenced a search for the stinker.

Within Penny's cabin were three sets of well-weathered work wear for weighty feet, a set of hunting boots, nicknamed Burger and Bun, and a pair of hiking shoes, dubbed Adam and Eve. My tennis shoes, a.k.a. Dumb and Dumber, remained tightly laced upon my feet. To this day, even with arthritic fingers, I continue to tie my shoes, avoiding Velcro closures, finding the harsh release rips to be vaguely reminiscent of a long-ago personal waxing.

Stretching ever so carefully to the floor behind Penny's passenger seat, ignoring traffic for a mere 15 seconds, I mustered Burger and Bun. Burger offered a drowsy oath, swearing on his shabby soul, asserting purity and implicating Bun as the likely carrier causing Penny's miasma. They both proved blameless but alas, to this day, Burger and Bun bunk in separate closets.

While employing my nimble knees to pilot Penny, I delved with my lithe arms behind her driver's seat. The left slinked between her door frame and seat as the right snaked across her center console and descended. Returning, they brought forth Adam and Eve who, in their innocence, made no excuse and were returned to their back-seat paradise.

Reclaiming my traffic lane and not wishing to endanger the public by removing Dumb and Dumber while in transit, I ducked beneath Penny's dashboard and skimmed my right index finger along Dumb's base. He was, at the time, engaged in spastic variations of Penny's speed unsettling the driver of the dump truck located just a lick off of Miss Purebred's derriere. Finding Dumb relatively clean, I lifted my left leg and set Dumber across my right knee.

While decoding the rearview mirror's image of the dump truck's license plate, DMPONU, and a bumper sticker which read, If U Can Read This Ur 2 Close, I changed the radio station with my left hand from Van Clyburn's performance of Rachmaninoff's *Second Piano Concerto* to Ozzy Osborn's speaker splitter, *No More Tears*, simultaneously wiping Dumber's bottom with my right hand.

Although my feet are as flat as a lefse griddle, Dumb and Dumber were manufactured with a comfortable arch support designed for those with the fortitude to jog the two blocks to the Dairy Queen. Hidden within Dumber's bottom side curvaceous cleavage was an odiferous glomp of doggy sludge, which transferred itself in gross to my unwary right hand. To no one in particular, I yelled, "Gack, get that crap off of me."

Within my camping supplies sack, strategically riding shotgun, there resides a plastic container of Wet Wipes, which have proven useful after leaving something behind for the deer to step in. As my starboard knee guided Penny within the traffic flow, my left hand reached across my body to search within the rucksack.

With my right hand elevated and my senses suffering from the stink, I leaned left and activated Penny's driver-side window lever with my nose. The Wet Wipes pack recovered and having successfully unclosed the window, I bit into the box top, unfastening the latch, and raised three perforated non-allergenic, unscented conscripts. Wait a minute. What beneficiary of their undertaking is allergic to perfume?

I entrusted my precious Penny to her own direction while I cleansed my sullied right hand and Dumber's sole. I pitched the gob of overburdened wipes out of the window and watched in Penny's side-view mirror as it caught an updraft and stuck onto the dump truck's windshield, midway up, driver's side.

Apropos, considering the license plate, the red-neck driver's baseball hat emblazoned with, Eat This, and his Sh-t Happens t-shirt. Red Neck activated the windshield Wet Wipes wipers, which captured its newest acquisition, smearing the wipe's contents hither and thither. Somewhat angered, the nincompoop attempted unsafe sex with Miss Purebred until he got off on County K.

For the remainder of our drive, I kept both hands upon Penny's steering wheel, both feet on her floor, and resisted the impulse to scratch anything or groom my nose.

I thought, "What a glorious day. Miss Penny Purebred and I own the road, a cloudless sky, and the fragrant breezes wafting though her windows; no more tears."

# # # # #

CASTE NOT

From the beginning of the human experience when the species *Homo sapiens* proved to be superior to the Neanderthals, so it was within our small-town grocery store as exhibited by the Produce Professionals versus the meat manglers (butchers).

At the onset of my career as a Produce Professional in 1966, Marv, my boss, the produce manager at our store, taught me about the grocery business caste system. We Produce Professionals maintain the top tier. Selling produce is a romance requiring an eye for freshness, color, display technique, sensitivity and beauty, the selfsame talents of a successful womanizer.

Occupying the descending levels of the system are grocery goofs who are mere can stackers. Then bakery buffoons, who work from recipes, which allows leeway for unplanned ingredients, such as cigarette butts, body hair, and various inedibles. Wednesday morning Big Po, our lead baker, lost his lower dentures and a well-kneaded wad of chewing tobacco into a batch of pumpernickel dough while laughing at a joke that only bakers would find funny. He retrieved his false teeth.

Next are the depraved dairy dorks and frozen food freaks, all of whom derive some kind of sick pleasure by chilling their body parts. Finally, owning the lowest level are the rank meat manglers, who spend their days eviscerating barnyard animals, chopping meat and creating heinous blood-spattered designs on their aprons, hats, boots, and innocent bystanders. According to Marv, most store managers won't interview candidates for a job in the meat department unless they have profuse body hair and knuckles that drag the ground. (Some meat manglers still have gill slits.)

A contingent of three manglers, a meat-wrapper shelf-stocker, and a trainee comprised the store's meat department. Most of them unintentionally bolstered Marv's classification. Karl, the manager, at about 45 years old, weighed at least a kiloton. Dale, aged in his late twenties, owned a sly smile, keen sense of humor and a wicked chopping arm.

Alfred, a skinny dude, was the perfect Laurel to Karl's Hardy. Alfred's height was difficult to judge due to his pronounced slouch. Mabel doubled as meat wrapper and shelf stocker. Her estimated age was between 65 and eternity as accentuated by her tightly wound bun hairstyle and ever present droopy cigarette. At the bottom rung of the rank was the apprentice, Two-Holer John. He was allotted the privilege of cleaning the slaughterhouse.

The contention between the highest and lowest caste, Produce Professionals and meat manglers, generated a myriad of practical jokes. Our ancient wooden produce cooler abutted the equally aged wooden meat storage locker. Over the top of the adjacent coolers was an attic that fashioned a corridor between the two backroom work areas. This passageway was a conduit for a diverse selection of missiles launched by the antagonists. For the voyage through the void to the meat backroom, Marv chose produce trash that guaranteed the utmost in explosive collateral damage: over-ripe tomatoes, peaches and cantaloupes, each with skins that barely contained their pulpy mass.

One particular direct hit is worthy of note. Marv heaved a hefty, rotten tomato over the coolers. It disintegrated upon impact like a water balloon on the back of Karl's neck, coating each hairy ridge in red tomato goop. Fortunately, meat by-products didn't lend themselves as well to distance, accuracy, and damage in retaliatory strikes. The cooler tops though, emanated the stench of their shortfall attempts. On this occasion, Karl proclaimed Marv's successful blow with a sonic boom of profanity.

On one particularly torrid July day, Marv ordered me to hide a 10-pound bag of spoiled, rotten russet potatoes—which produce the most pungent scent in the produce business—beneath the front passenger seat of Dale's clunker and roll up the windows as best I could. Subsequent to the bag's discovery and disposal, Dale's car windows remained at ebb tide through the next three thunderstorms and yet the aroma remained.

Dale retaliated by stashing a container of beef liver in the furnace vent above our produce workbench. Eventually, Marv located the source of the stink and complimented himself in that it wasn't personally generated as accused by Dale.

In the continuing spiral of retaliatory strikes, Marv assigned another mission, no matter if I was willing to accept it. I obtained an aluminum tray used for wrapped meat storage, opened the swinging door to the meat mausoleum, and pitched that tray as high and far as possible. It floated, stalled momentarily in time, then clanged upon their band saw, bounced over a personally soiled meat mangler, and managed three skips along the floor. Language never before heard by the common customer generated a sound wave that is yet traveling towards the S.E.T.I. projects of undiscovered worlds.

Marv had a penchant for fine-looking women. At my age of 16 years, I was not fully attuned to the nuances of female admiration. Marv took full responsibility for my tutelage. Within a few months of my hiring, I learned more about girls than I had since my creation.

Our assistant store manager, Mike, hired a busty young lady to offer samples of a clear soda pop, Bubble Up, to our customers. Mike excitedly invited Marv and me to a gathering in the grocery backroom. Upon entering, we found a semi-circular wall of stacked toilet tissue boxes. The partial enclosure was inhabited by the comely soda pop lady demonstrating products and services, in which I had never indulged nor imagined. Mike and Marv took turns partaking behind the enclosure.

While resting from their sampling, they insisted that I partake. Life-threatening circumstances beget a choice: fright, fight or flight. I chose all three as my frightened fight to escape nearly toppled Dale, who was leading the train of meat manglers towards the demonstration facility. Even though unaccustomed to life outside of the meat department, I felt confident that their safe return would be guided by their telltale trail of bloody sawdust foot prints.

Marv claimed to have invented the customer "Babe I.D." system, an in-store program to announce the presence of attractive women shoppers. They would be classified per sex appeal on a scale of 1 to 10, dog to eye-popper. Marv demonstrated his system thusly: he spotted a fine-looking babe in aisle #4 and announced over the loudspeaker, "94 cents on that item, Karl." The first number designated the woman's grade on the 1-to-10 scale. The second number, the aisle of her location, and the name reference, Karl, indicated that she was close to the meat department. Fortunately for the numbering system, our store had but nine grocery aisles accompanied by produce, bakery, dairy, frozen food, and meat departments.

Meat manglers are a reclusive lot of anchorites, shunning the public and store employees. They spend their time behind closed doors, smoking, swearing, spitting, slipping on sawdust, and slicing some meat. No one wished to venture within their gory grotto. One and only one enticement would induce an exodus of the hermits from their den of horrors—a babe rating greater than 6.

Our store was located on the edge of the ritzy Lake Minnetonka district. Our shoppers consisted of a nice mix of farmers, and the social elite who could afford a fancy country home on the shores of the lake. On this glorious summer day, Marv's "94 cents" announcement identified a young lady customer from the lakeshore who was parading in her steamy 1960s bikini. All the butchers, except Karl, escaped the backroom as if there was a tornado alert. Karl was last to leave due to his weight-impeded gait and his girth that made egress through the backroom door a challenge.

All were now craftily stationed in aisle #4. Not one man had bothered to remove his bloodied uniform. Each mangler went about straightening cans on the grocery shelves, depositing bloody finger prints with every positioning. (Meat manglers are known for their 270-degree peripheral vision when viewing high-grade meat or women.) A few minutes into the rush, the lady's husband arrived and was clever enough to ascertain the reason for the crowd. Madam was unceremoniously removed from their presence and the store, sans groceries, while Monsieur generated a cumulonimbus cloud of expletives that to this day storms over Lake Minnetonka.

As watching the meat manglers' hurried dance to leave their slaughterhouse hermitage was a favorite pastime for Marv and the perfect practical joke, Marv often placed a fake announcement over the airwaves. The manglers could not afford to disregard the broadcast and risk missing an excellent viewing. Karl was frequently caught exiting just as the others were returning.

Progress has its disadvantages. Today's grocery megamarkets lack the intimacy required for rivalries between the elite Produce Professionals and the few remaining meat manglers. The "Babe I.D." system has fallen by the wayside as prices for modest items are well beyond the system's required two decimal points, and grocery stores contain scores of aisles and departments. A "Babe I.D." system would require a logarithmic calculator. Now, more than forty years later, while grocery shopping, an infrequent announcement of a price just below a dollar yet evokes memories of high-priced babes and cheap practical jokes.

# # # # #

Special Occasions

My wife, Cora, doesn't care for my wardrobe. I don't understand her problem. All that I own is highly functional.

I have eight pairs of accomplished blue jeans and one black pair for special occasions, six seasoned, long-sleeved, sky-blue shirts and one white shirt for special occasions, four pairs of veteran military boots, three tan suede and one black for special occasions, two pairs of broken-in tennis shoes, one white and one black for special occasions, a dozen pair of mature socks, ten white and two black (yes, that's right) and four each of mostly white undershirts and jockey shorts, all for special occasions.

This limited, yet tasteful, selection allows me to sleep in thirty minutes longer than Cora and still get dressed before she has finished choosing her attire. If, perchance, I lay out my clothes the night before, add two minutes to that number.

From one day to next, I'm recognizable, blue on blue, (now I'm humming that song, again) except on special occasions. Whether I'm planning to labor at the workplace or in our forest, dine out or visit friends, I'm good to go.

Cora is certain to point out each and every time-honored defect in my clothing, unlike the rest of humanity, all of whom understand that such is expected from a man of many talents. She's threatened to sort through my 10% share of our clothing closet and my dresser drawer and dispose of all the items that have seen their day. That's okay by me. I don't mind being naked. Thus far, that thought alone has short-circuited her bullying.

This morning, she commanded, "Go change your blue jeans. There's a hole in your butt (no comment). I can see your underwear."

My first thought was, "If she had a hole in her clothing, I'd keep my mouth shut and enjoy the view."

My second thought, "What hole? I can't see any hole, under where?"

My second and third second thoughts, "I'm wearing underwear? What's the special occasion?"

#####

Afterthoughts

I said to Cora, "I'm going to wear a blue shirt to the wedding."

Cora replied, "I'm thinking a white shirt."

I rejoined, "Think what you want. I like the blue."

Cora rebutted, "You can wear a white shirt to the wedding or a blue shirt to your funeral."

###

I mentioned to Cora that we'll be blowing bubbles at the wedding, instead of throwing rice. She replied, "The only bubbles you know how to blow are in the bathtub."

###

I noticed a headline in our newspaper, "Church Briefs." I don't want to see those.

###

Whoever invented the word loveseat for a small couch must have been unmarried.

###

The Buzz

For some reason, nearly every morning since my retirement and simultaneous designation as a humble house husband, about half an hour after breakfast, I find myself beset by a tremendous surge of energy. I call it "The Buzz." I can't control the rapidity of my actions, the number of tasks I tackle, or the distractions.

Wednesday at 7:30 a.m., shortly after breakfast, I abandoned the morning newspaper mid-story, something about Lindsay Lohan, and began my morning chores in earnest. I dumped our laundry bin's contents onto our unmade queen-size bed and sorted the soiled attire into pattern piles: stripes, plaids and solids. I read somewhere, maybe in *O Magazine*, that laundry should be sorted before washing.

While so engaged, I found a goblet on Cora's nightstand. Cora "the Dish" is my employed, full-blooded Norwegian wife. I gulped the two inches of white wine that remained and raced the emptied glass into the kitchen for placement in our dishwasher.

The dishwasher's disheveled shelves looked far from full. I rearranged their contents and scouted the tops of the stove, kitchen counter, night stands, dining table, and TV room tables for prospective bathers. After watching several minutes of *The Price is Right* and departing before the showcase results, I dashed to the kitchen and placed the dishes, silverware, and drinking glasses I had found into the tidy dishwasher. There yet remained a few unfilled slots on the bottom shelf. I reached into the dinnerware cabinet and recruited three sparkling volunteers from the selection to complete the load.

I poured powdered dish detergent into the washer's soap slots, and for an instant, flashed back to the telltale beverage blotches on the various tops. I tore off a couple paper towels from the roll and grabbed the spray counter cleaner container from beneath the sink. I quickly cleansed the splotches, smashing my shin on the unclosed dishwasher door in the process.

As the door doddered, the open soap slots sprayed their contents onto the inside of the washer door and the kitchen floor below. I hustled to the closet and snatched the broom and dust pan, but couldn't tear myself away when I beheld a stocking cap and a pair of gloves on the floor, our plastic grocery bag full of plastic grocery bags tipped over, two of Cora's jackets on my side of the closet, and several coats hung with their fronts facing left. I picked up the cap and gloves, righted the bag of bags, reinstated the Dish's coats, and reoriented the closet clothing.

Plastic bags, serendipity! I retrieved one and made a bee-line for the waste basket beneath the kitchen sink. I removed the burgeoning bag of trash that was overflowing the basket and replaced it with the empty bag. There, on the counter, waited the dish detergent box. I set the bulging trash bag down for a second and latched onto the soap box.

Without delay, I refilled the soap slots, closed their doors and the washer door, activated the bugger, returned the counter cleaner and the soap box to their proper positions beneath the sink, and tripped over the burdened bag, scattering its contents hither and thither.

Employing the broom and dust pan, I made short work of the ejected garbage and powdered dish detergent. I returned the tools to their designated resting place in the closet and speedily transported the bursting bag to the trash container in the garage.

I noticed the dried tree leaves strewn all about the garage floor and shot back inside to retrieve the broom. While swiftly sweeping, I caught sight of a motor oil glob upon the garage floor where Cora's car rests overnight. With no time to locate a rag, I blotted the oil glob with my handkerchief.

Not wanting to stuff the stained cloth into my pants pocket, I set the broom aside momentarily and motored indoors to the laundry mounds on our bed. I didn't have a load designated for polka dots, but because Oprah wasn't watching, I buried my sullied handkerchief within the plaids pile and rushed that heap to the washing machine.

As I quick-stepped through the basement laundry room, I disturbed a dozen or so laundry-lint dust bunnies on the tile floor. I laid the plaids atop the washing machine and warped back up to the garage to reclaim the broom.

For mercy's sake, stop! It's 9:30 a.m. and I am already breathless, even though the garage and laundry room floors lie in wait to be swept, and the plaids on the washer and the stripes and solids upon our unmade bed wish to be washed. OMG, I … I can't stand it. I've got to finish those jobs in order as listed. I'll be right back.

It is 12:30 p.m. There's time for a peanut butter and marshmallow cream sandwich while I finish reading the morning newspaper. I'm pleased to report that the floors are swept, the laundry is done, and the bed is made. And my car, Ms. Penny Purebred, is nearly washed, the laundry room cabinets are almost straightened, and the bedroom is just about vacuumed.

I hereby resolve not to repeat this habitual frenzy tomorrow morning or for that matter any other morning in the foreseeable future. Perhaps a change in the sugar and caffeine content of my breakfast menu may be of assistance.

Thursday I didn't shower C&H Pure Cane Sugar from Hawaii on my boatload of Captain Crunch. The Captain's cereal was still satisfying, and I felt a bit calmer for a fleeting interval. Tomorrow I'll make use of the same strategy with my Frosted Flakes.

Saturday, no sugar sprinkled on my Quisp. Sunday, I'll cut back to two pieces of white bread toast awash in my sister-in-law's thick homemade plum jelly. Yes, at the risk of shipwreck, I'm proceeding at flank speed to overcome "The Buzz." Monday I'll down a tumbler of orange juice with breakfast instead of my customary can of Classic Coke.

# # # # #

AFTERTHOUGHT

After two glasses of wine, Cora said, "You're starting to look good to me."

I crowed, "Yesssssssss, I've still got it!"

# # #

Acknowledgments

Thanks to my wife Cora, family, and friends for their continued contributions to my writings and to my sister, Rhonda Hadlock, for her efforts to edit them.

# # # # #

Cora and Rick Wehler at Devil's Lake State Park (2011)

ABOUT THE AUTHOR

Rick and Cora Wehler are retired and live in Sun Prairie, Wisconsin. They have three sons and are now enjoying five grandchildren. Rick and Cora are true Minne-Sconsinites, having lived over thirty years in each state.

If you'd like to contact Rick, please email him at:
northofnormal@thewehlers.com

Cora and Rick Wehler at Rhonda and Terry Hadlock's wedding (January 2008)

CPSIA information can be obtained
at www.ICGtesting.com
Printed in the USA
FFOW04n2244280716
26316FF